The City:
A World History

The New Oxford World History

The City:
A World History

Andrew Lees

OXFORD
UNIVERSITY PRESS

OXFORD
UNIVERSITY PRESS

Oxford University Press is a department of the University of
Oxford. It furthers the University's objective of excellence in research,
scholarship, and education by publishing worldwide.

Oxford   New York
Auckland   Cape Town   Dar es Salaam   Hong Kong   Karachi
Kuala Lumpur   Madrid   Melbourne   Mexico City   Nairobi
New Delhi   Shanghai   Taipei   Toronto

With offices in
Argentina   Austria   Brazil   Chile   Czech Republic   France   Greece
Guatemala   Hungary   Italy   Japan   Poland   Portugal   Singapore
South Korea   Switzerland   Thailand   Turkey   Ukraine   Vietnam

Oxford is a registered trademark of Oxford University Press
in the UK and certain other countries.

Published in the United States of America by
Oxford University Press
198 Madison Avenue, New York, NY 10016

Library of Congress Cataloging-in-Publication Data
Lees, Andrew, 1940–
The city : a world history / Andrew Lees.
pages cm. — (New Oxford world history)
Includes bibliographical references and index.
ISBN 978–0–19–985954–2 (pbk. : alk. paper); ISBN 978–0–19–985952–8 (hardback : alk. paper)
1. Cities and towns—History.   2. Cities and towns—Growth—History.   I. Title.
HT111.L44 2015
307.7609—dc23
2015003459

*Frontispiece: The Petronas Twin Towers in Malaysia's Kuala Lumpur, at
1,483 feet, are the tallest twin towers in the world, but their height is exceeded
by several other single skyscrapers. Skyscrapers were invented in Chicago in the
late nineteenth century and became widespread in New York City early in the
twentieth century.* Photo by Craig Lockard.

For Lynn,
my beloved companion during many years
in learning and in life

Contents

Editors' Preface

This book is part of the New Oxford World History, an innovative series that offers readers an informed, lively, and up-to-date history of the world and its people that represents a significant change from the "old" world history. Only a few years ago, world history generally amounted to a history of the West—Europe and the United States—with small amounts of information from the rest of the world. Some versions of the "old" world history drew attention to every part of the world *except* Europe and the United States. Readers of that kind of world history could get the impression that somehow the rest of the world was made up of exotic people who had strange customs and spoke difficult languages. Still another kind of "old" world history presented the story of areas or peoples of the world by focusing primarily on the achievements of great civilizations. One learned of great buildings, influential world religions, and mighty rulers but little of ordinary people or more general economic and social patterns. Interactions among the world's peoples were often told from only one perspective.

This series tells world history differently. First, it is comprehensive, covering all countries and regions of the world and investigating the total human experience—even those of so-called peoples without histories living far from the great civilizations. "New" world historians thus share in common an interest in all of human history, even going back millions of years before there were written human records. A few "new" world histories even extend their focus to the entire universe, a "big history" perspective that dramatically shifts the beginning of the story back to the big bang. Some see the "new" global framework of world history today as viewing the world from the vantage point of the moon, as one scholar put it. We agree. But we also want to take a close-up view, analyzing and reconstructing the significant experiences of all of humanity.

This is not to say that everything that has happened everywhere and in all time periods can be recovered or is worth knowing, but that there is much to be gained by considering both the separate and interrelated stories of different societies and cultures. Making these connections is still another crucial ingredient of the "new" world history. It emphasizes connectedness and interactions of all kinds—cultural, economic, political, religious, and social—involving peoples, places, and processes. It makes comparisons and finds similarities. Emphasizing both the comparisons and interactions is critical to developing a global framework that can deepen and broaden historical understanding, whether the focus is on a specific country or region or on the whole world.

The rise of the new world history as a discipline comes at an opportune time. The interest in world history in schools and among the general public is vast. We travel to one another's nations, converse and work with people around the world, and are changed by global events. War and peace affect populations worldwide, as do economic conditions and the state of our environment, communications, and health and medicine. The New Oxford World History presents local histories in a global context and gives an overview of world events seen through the eyes of ordinary people. This combination of the local and the global further defines the new world history. Understanding the workings of global and local conditions in the past gives us tools for examining our own world and for envisioning the interconnected future that is in the making.

Bonnie G. Smith
Anand Yang

CHAPTER 1

Origins and Locations of Early Cities, 3500–500 BCE

The earliest cities arose for the most part independently of one another in several parts of the world, beginning around the middle of the fourth millennium BCE, and despite some setbacks, their growth has continued up to the present. Cities emerged from the countryside as new forms of human settlements, whose inhabitants lived under conditions quite different from those of their predecessors and rural contemporaries. Despite the fact that they long contained only a small minority of the world's population, they have had profound impacts on the societies in which they have arisen. They have enormously enhanced city dwellers' capabilities and powerfully promoted innovations of all sorts—technological, political, cultural, and intellectual. The advances that have taken place in cities have fostered comparable development among residents of the hinterlands that surrounded them, serving as powerful stimuli that have helped to drive the development of civilization in general. In fact, the word "civilization" is derived from the Latin *civitas*, which originally meant "city-state."

This is not to say that the rise and impact of cities have always been beneficial. In addition to exacerbating myriad problems in areas of both public health and social (or antisocial) behavior, cities have served as headquarters for the progenitors of war and conquest. The rise of these forces has also been an important part of the story of enhanced capabilities. The urban factor has loomed exceedingly large as a determinant of other aspects of human history, way out of proportion to the size of cities, either territorially or demographically. Marked by both benefits and deficits that have elicited lavish praise or abundant criticism, cities have embodied powerful motor forces in the development of humankind.

What was (and is) a city? Historians and other scholars generally agree on several features as defining characteristics of urban settlements. For an area to count as urban in the eyes of historians, it has to have been marked by both a relatively high density of population and a relatively large population. While the statistical cutoffs have changed as overall population has grown, even quite dense settlements that, in ancient times, comprised only a few hundred inhabitants are usually designated as villages rather than as cities. Thus, size does matter. Cities must be relatively compact and relatively big.

Cities have also exhibited a high degree of durability. Over a millennium after Uruk, the first great city known to us, was founded, the wall that surrounded it and its main temple were glowingly described in a long anonymous poem that is known as the *Epic of Gilgamesh* (a god to which the city supposedly owed its birth):

> Of ramparted Uruk the wall he built,
> Of hallowed Eanna [a temple] the pure sanctuary.
> Behold its outer wall, whose cornice is like copper,
> Peer at the inner wall, which none can equal!
> Seize upon the threshold, which is from of old!
> Draw near to Eanna, the dwelling of Ishtar [a goddess],
> Which no future king, no man, can equal.
> Go up and walk on the walls of Uruk,
> Inspect the base terrace, examine the brickwork:
> Is not its brickwork of burnt brick?
> Did not the Seven [Sages] lay its foundations?[1]

The poet expresses awe for the wondrous splendor of a mighty city—a sentiment reiterated often in later centuries by champions of urban settlements.

To be sure, cities have waxed and waned, sometimes declining sharply either as a result of economic forces or because of military assaults. But they have displayed a much higher degree of physical permanence—in the form of streets, buildings, and other structures—than has been evident elsewhere. (Cities were also often set apart, during both the early and later parts of their existences, from what lay outside them by protective walls, although in recent centuries, such structures have almost entirely disappeared, and even when they have not vanished, they no longer demarcate a city's outer boundaries.)

Finally, although cities' legal and political status has varied widely, some sort of urban government, whether controlled from above by a hereditary ruler or an oligarchy or controlled from below by a wider portion of the citizenry, has also usually been part of the picture. (Identifying a particular city as the area located within the boundaries of a legally defined municipality simplifies the task of distinguishing between the city itself and what lies outside of it. Some urbanists, however, include built-up areas that extend far beyond urban municipalities as parts of cities, referring, for instance, to a "Greater" New York that is home to twice as many people as the approximately 8.4 million New Yorkers who live in the five boroughs.)

Although all cities share certain features, there have been numerous types of cities. Many of the most enduring ones have served as administrative cities—as political capitals. Others (often located on rivers or near oceans) have served as centers of trade and commerce. Then there are the cities that have been centers of industry, religion, or culture. Some cities have arisen quickly as a result of decisions made by a political ruler, whereas many more have arisen gradually as results of decisions made by individuals. Heterogeneity has been one of the most salient features of urban places and urban life.

The emergence and the growth of cities have depended heavily on transformations in rural areas. Urban settlements could never have arisen without vast changes in the ways in which people obtained food. The essential precondition for the growth of cities was a shift from Old Stone Age hunting and foraging, with arrows and spears, to Neolithic or New Stone Age agriculture, with sharp stone axes to cut down trees, stone-bladed hoes to till land cleared for cultivation, bone or wooden sickles to harvest grain, and mortars and pestles to turn grain into flour. Neolithic people also used flint knives to kill animals for food and clothing. The shift took thousands of years, starting sometime in the ninth or tenth millennium BCE and spreading to most parts of the world by about 4000 BCE. Later, between about 4000 BCE and 2500 BCE, the use of copper in the alloy bronze made the production of the first metal tools possible, including plowshares and also sharper axes and knives.

These technological developments enabled people to grow crops and raise livestock such as cattle, sheep, and chickens for meat, milk, and eggs. By growing and raising what they ate instead of finding and catching it, they exchanged nomadic ways of living (which were often necessitated by the depletion of local sources of food) for more permanent settlements. In addition, for the first time, human beings were able to produce more than they needed to eat.

Now certain sectors of society—freed from the need to produce their own food—could turn to nonagricultural pursuits. Division of labor became increasingly widespread. Demographic density helped to foster a variety of specialized activities. People became more engaged in the making of nonedible goods (e.g., better and better tools that generated still-greater agricultural surpluses) and other forms of nonagricultural labor. Not only manufacturing and buying and selling of goods but also governmental administration and the orchestration of religious ceremonies took hold. Early governments, ruled by kings and staffed by men who specialized in the maintenance of written records, grew up in large part to ensure that the agricultural surpluses now required by urban elites and other city dwellers would be provided on favorable terms. Priests helped to foster the belief that rulers' coercive powers were divinely sanctioned, and warriors also backed up governmental compulsion with the exercise or threat of force.

Because the earliest cities sprang up before the rise of long-distance commerce in foodstuffs, they had to be located relatively close to areas where the food surpluses on which they depended were produced. Because agriculture required ample supplies of water and also because the most economical way for cities to receive imports was via water, early cities were often located in river valleys, downstream from where agricultural production took place. Being downstream facilitated the shipment of goods that were usually bulkier and heavier than whatever goods city dwellers sent upstream in exchange for the food they imported, thus minimizing the costs of interregional transportation. It also facilitated trade along seashores, which contributed further to the economic specialization that urban development required.

These preconditions were first met in Southwest Asia, in an area roughly contiguous with today's Iraq and the northern part of Syria. The ancient Greeks called the area "Mesopotamia," or "between the rivers," namely the Tigris and Euphrates rivers. Now a relatively barren area from the standpoint of agriculture, in ancient times, this territory enjoyed abundant supplies of water and highly fertile soil. As its inhabitants figured out ways to control periodic flooding and to direct water via canals into areas where and when it was wanted, agricultural production increased steadily.

The need for social and political organization to manage the flow of water and ensure the extraction of agricultural surpluses played a key part in the creation of Mesopotamian cities. Urban settlements that were for the most part politically independent and thus functioned as city-states began to appear in large numbers around the middle of the fourth millennium BCE. One of the first about which we have solid information was the city of Uruk, which has been extensively excavated by archaeologists. Located in the southern part of Mesopotamia in an area known as Sumer, it grew from about 300 acres in 3600 BCE to

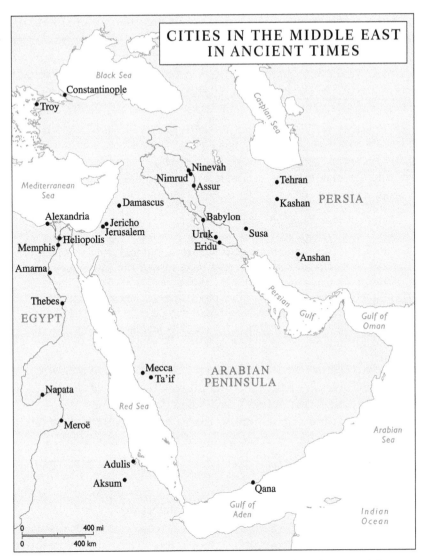

CITIES IN THE MIDDLE EAST IN ANCIENT TIMES

Black Sea

Constantinople

Troy

Caspian Sea

Mediterranean Sea

Ninevah

Nimrud • Assur

• Tehran

Damascus

• Kashan PERSIA

Alexandria

• Jericho
Jerusalem

Babylon

Heliopolis

Uruk • Susa
Eridu •

Memphis

• Anshan

Amarna

Thebes •

EGYPT

Persian

Gulf

Gulf of Oman

Mecca
• Ta'if

ARABIAN
PENINSULA

Napata

Red Sea

Arabian Sea

Meroë

Adulis •

Aksum •

Qana

Gulf of Aden

Indian Ocean

0 ————— 400 mi
0 ————— 400 km

Cities first arose in Southwest Asia several millennia before the start of the Christian Era. Places such as Uruk were concentrated at first in the fertile valley of the Tigris and Euphrates rivers. They arose in later centuries in other parts of the region, from Kashan in Persia to Troy and Constantinople in what is now Turkey, and from there to Thebes in Egypt. Based on a map by Niko Lipsanen.

more than seven times that size by 2800 BCE. Already by 3200 BCE, Uruk had a population of around 20,000 inhabitants, making it the largest city in this part of the world, and by 2800 BCE, its population may have been as high as 50,000.

During the period of about three millennia that began around the founding of Uruk, numerous other cities arose in Mesopotamia, both in Sumer and to the north in areas known as Babylonia and Assyria. Eridu, Ur, Lagash, Nippur, Kish (which between 2500 and 2000 BCE may have had a population of 60,000), and Nineveh flourished as urban societies. The one city that stood out among all the others in Mesopotamia by about 600 BCE was one of the grandest of all the cities in the ancient world: Babylon. The ancient Greek historian Herodotus, in his fifth-century BCE *History*, was mightily impressed by both its size and its magnificence (though his measurements were no doubt exaggerated):

> Assyria possesses a vast number of great cities, whereof the most renowned and strongest at this time was Babylon. . . . The city stands on a broad plain, and is an exact square, a hundred and twenty furlongs in length [fifteen miles] each way, so that the entire circuit is four hundred and eighty furlongs [sixty miles]. While such is its size, in magnificence there is no other city that approaches to it. It is surrounded, in the first place, by a broad and deep moat, full of water, behind which rises a wall fifty royal cubits [about eighty-seven feet] in width, and two hundred in height.[2]

In the sixth century BCE, Babylon served as the capital of a Babylonian kingdom, headed by King Nebuchadnezzar II, that had flourished as an ally of Medes from the north, who had destroyed most of the cities in Assyria. With a population on the order of 200,000 to 300,000 inhabitants, it could lay claim to being the first of the world's giant cities. Approachable only by a processional way sixty-three feet wide and more than 1,000 feet long, at the end of which one passed through the forty-foot-high Ishtar Gate, the city was surrounded by a double wall so wide that chariots could travel along its top.

Mesopotamian cities' architectural features set them distinctly apart from areas outside of them. City walls, which were often behind defensive moats, served in the first place as means of defense; but they also served as means of inculcating into the minds of inhabitants and visitors alike a sense of a city's grandeur and power that would, it was hoped, both cultivate loyalty and discourage would-be assailants. Within a city's walls, the most impressive building was the city's main temple. Platforms that raised temples above all other buildings were intended to convey a sense of ascension toward heaven as one entered the temple. Dedicated to the worship of one or another deity, temples also provided spaces in which craftsmen who were employed by priests plied their trades—whether

Named after a goddess of love and fertility, the Gate of Ishtar was built about 575 BCE as a point of entry in a wall that surrounded the mighty city of Babylon, at that time the largest city in the world. A reconstruction of the gate can be seen today in the Pergamon Museum in Berlin. Bpk, Berlin/Vorderasiatisches Museum/Art Resource, NY, ART315855.

as weavers, potters, or jewelers—and in which scribes and teachers, as well as bureaucrat-priests, went about their business. In addition to temples, royal palaces also stood out on the urban scene, bearing witness to the authority possessed by kings, who were often regarded as semi-divine. Otherwise, most of the structures in these cities consisted of small one-story houses along narrow alleys. These cities, like later ones, embodied a high degree of social inequality that their structures made quite clear.

Although palaces proclaimed the powerful positions of royal rulers, whose importance rose as increasingly larger territories (e.g., the Babylonian Kingdom and the Assyrian Empire) subsumed formerly independent city-states, urban life also fostered self-government. Popular assemblies of citizens, some of which possessed authority throughout cities while others functioned within smaller districts, had originated for the purpose of serving as law courts that handled both civil and criminal cases. Over time, members of these assemblies likely sought to play a greater part in local government. Whether they succeeded in this regard or not, the assemblies did serve as venues for discussion and debate about matters of public concern. Activities that occurred within these institutions led, moreover, to the emergence of new groups of officials who served as intermediaries between the citizenry and kings. Pressures coming from these officials, as well as from the assemblies, helped city dwellers gain exemptions from obligations that fell on inhabitants of the countryside, particularly with regard to taxation and military service.

Men who lived in Mesopotamian cities played a key part in the invention of writing, for which these cities served as early incubators. Already by the end of the fourth millennium BCE, scribes who worked under the direction of public authorities made use of a system of writing known as cuneiform, which combined alphabetical and pictographic elements. The invention of cuneiform greatly facilitated the organization of urban life. Inscribing words on clay tablets, the scribes produced records that governments needed in order to keep track of their own and citizens' rights and obligations. The law code proclaimed by the Babylonian King Hammurabi in the eighteenth century BCE stands out as one of the oldest documents of significant length that has ever been deciphered. It consists of 282 separate laws dealing with a wide range of matters, among them wages for various kinds of work, the liabilities of builders of collapsed houses, household and family relationships, inheritance rights, sexual behavior, and obligations to perform military service. The code also indicated harsh punishments for breaking these laws, according to the principle of "an eye for an eye, a tooth for a tooth." Although most of what was written pertained to laws and administration, many documents recorded commercial transactions. Others served religious purposes, taking shape as prayers, hymns, or prescriptions for rituals. Beyond the texts that had to do with governmental, economic, and religious matters, many others embodied intellectual and cultural production in the areas of science, mathematics, medicine, history, and literature.

As the establishment of cities proceeded in Mesopotamia, comparable developments began to occur in other places that had also benefited from the Neolithic Revolution, both near Mesopotamia and as far away as East Asia and Latin America. Roughly between the third millennium and the middle of the first millennium BCE, contiguous settlements that numbered 10,000 or more inhabitants, possessing many of the qualities that characterized their predecessors in Mesopotamia, appeared. In some instances, urban development took place in connection with trading relationships between urban and nonurban areas that led to the export, or at least emulation, of urban forms. Just as networks of cities developed within regions, cities could also develop trans-regionally, as people who lived in relatively advanced areas established urban colonies and set examples that (some) inhabitants of relatively backward areas followed. Still, for the most part, the establishment of cities took place autonomously. Albeit at widely varying times, many cities evolved without the benefit of external influences. A capacity for city-building became apparent among people who inhabited most if not all of the world's continents.

Both sorts of urban development led to the rise of urban settlements in half a dozen areas outside ancient Mesopotamia, to its south and west and from Southwest Asia to East Asia. To Mesopotamia's southwest, there arose a separate civilization that nonetheless bore the imprint of Sumerian influences. Straddling the Nile River over a distance of 600 miles from a cataract at Aswan in the south to the Nile Delta in the north, the several kingdoms of Egypt (the first of which was founded around 3100 BCE when a conqueror named Menes succeeded in unifying Upper and Lower Egypt) benefited not only agriculturally from the Nile's annual flooding. They were also, quite possibly, beneficiaries of the results of commercial exchanges that went back and forth along a maritime route from the Persian Gulf around Arabia and up the Red Sea. Whatever the paths that led to commercial interactions, it seems that Mesopotamian methods of construction (particularly the use of bricks) and also the practice of writing with pictographs, as well as the production of copper, may well have traveled from Sumer to Egypt. Sumerian influences thus likely contributed to the rise of Egyptian cities in a variety of ways.

Nonetheless, Egyptian cities differed considerably from the ones that had emerged in Mesopotamia. Places such as Memphis (established by Menes shortly after he took power) and Thebes (established well to the south of Memphis as a seat of rule by a new dynasty that began around 2050 BCE) were relatively small in comparison with their Mesopotamian counterparts. Moreover, unlike early Mesopotamian cities, they were not city-states. They functioned instead as capitals of the territorial states in which they were located. Their geographic isolation spared them the threat of assaults by armies from nearby city-states; they did not need to be fortified, and consequently they were not surrounded by walls. Inside the cities, commercial and manufacturing activity was relatively rudimentary. Memphis, Thebes, and other Egyptian cities that served as provincial capitals were primarily administrative and religious centers, not centers of economic activity, and their leading citizens were bureaucrats and priests, not merchants. Still, even if it did not produce great wealth, Thebes displayed it. With its large and splendid palace, its temples, its many tombs for kings and noblemen, and a population by about 1400 BCE of around 50,000 to 80,000, it appeared in the eyes of its inhabitants to be a great metropolis. One of them praised it as the archetypical urban place: "she is called the city; all others are under her shadow, to magnify themselves through her."[3] Cities elsewhere in Africa before 500 BCE appeared mainly just to the south of Egypt. In the second millennium BCE, the small city of Kerma in present-day Sudan served as the capital of a Kerman Kingdom until this territory became an Egyptian colony.

The Egyptian cities of Thebes, Tiryns, and Pylos occupied important positions in a commercial empire that radiated from the city of Mycenae in present-day Greece and reached its height between about 1400 and 1200 BCE. Starting no later than the end of the second millennium BCE, cities had begun to emerge on the Greek mainland and on islands in the eastern part of the Mediterranean in areas inhabited by Greeks. Some of the earliest city builders were people who had migrated into the area from the north. Noteworthy for their complex and heavy fortifications and their palaces, Mycenaean cities went nonetheless into eclipse—possibly after another invasion from the north around 1000 BCE by Greeks who were known as Dorians—and their legacy to other cities in the Aegean area was not substantial.

During the third millennium BCE, cities also began to spring up on the eastern shores of the Mediterranean in a small portion of what is now Lebanon and Syria that was known as Phoenicia. One of the first of these cities was Byblos, a coastal town with seafaring inhabitants who supported themselves not by conquest but entirely by means of commerce. Merchants who were based there engaged in trade, not only in Southwest Asia but as far away as the Caucasus and the Sudan. In subsequent centuries, numerous other cities emerged in the region, among them Beirut, Acre, Sidon, and Tyre. Like Byblos, these cities were located on the Mediterranean coast, from which their inhabitants launched vessels for long-distance trade. Phoenician merchants exported cedar, glass, jewelry, and woven cloth, bringing back foodstuffs and raw materials from foreign ports to be used in manufacturing. Their cities were not among the largest in the region. At their height, between about 1200 and 700 BCE, none of them exceeded 30,000 inhabitants, but they stood out in the area for their prosperity and their splendor.

The most celebrated of the Phoenician cities was Tyre, whose praises the biblical prophet Ezekiel sang:

> Your borders are in the heart of the seas; your builders made perfect your beauty. They made all your planks of fir trees from Senir [Mount Hermon]; they took a cedar from Lebanon to make a mast for you. Of oaks of Bashan [east of the Sea of Galilee] they made your oars; they made your deck of pines from the coasts of Cyprus, inlaid with fine ivory. Of fine embroidered linen from Egypt was your sail. . . . All the ships of the sea with their mariners were in you, to barter for your wares.[4]

The Phoenicians not only founded cities at home but also carried out a colonizing process abroad, making their mark far to the west. They established port colonies in a number of places that later became cities in their own right, most notably Carthage (which became the dominant city in the western Mediterranean by the end of the fifth century BCE) in northern Africa, Palermo on the island of Sicily, and Cadiz in Spain. At the same time, they took the lead in developing a phonetic alphabet. It greatly facilitated the keeping of written records, which were increasingly important foundations of urban life.

Stimuli that came from Southwest Asia may also have contributed, via trade, to the further urban growth that occurred in South Asia, starting in what is now Pakistan. Benefiting both agriculturally and commercially from the mighty Indus River, inhabitants of the area came together in several cities that existed in the Indus Valley approximately between 2500 and 1500 BCE. The major cities in this area, Harappa and Mohenjo-Daro, served as capitals of a Harappan Empire that stretched over hundreds of miles. They were relatively large from a spatial standpoint. Around 2000 BCE, each comprised about 40,000 inhabitants living in an area of about a square mile. Unlike cities in Mesopotamia, they were carefully laid out according to common ground plans, which showed that they had been carefully designed, very likely at the behest of a single ruler. Streets were constructed according to grid patterns; there was a fortified citadel at the western edge of each city; there were wells and bathhouses; and there were complex drainage systems. These cities were also surrounded by embankments intended to provide protection from floods. About 1500 BCE, the Harappan Empire fell victim to Sanskrit-speaking Aryan invaders who moved into the area from Central Asia. As a result of both this change and other, natural factors (such as declining rainfall and river shifts), cities in the Indus Valley soon went into sharp decline. Much later, to the southeast, the rise of several kingdoms was accompanied around 500 BCE by the growth of new towns along the Ganges River. Soon thereafter, the establishment of the Mauryan Empire, which ruled over most of India between the fourth and first centuries BCE, also led to the prospering of urban centers, exemplified by the affluence of the capital, Pataliputra, and also such places as Ayodhya and Benares.

Although there were some commercial contacts between South Asia and East Asia, urbanization in China must be regarded as a largely independent development. While there is some evidence of cities that originated as early as 3000 BCE, most historians begin their accounts of Chinese urban history with developments that occurred between the eighteenth and third centuries BCE during the Shang and Zhou dynasties. The first cities arose in northern China near the Yellow River. The most prominent of these settlements was Yin, the Shang capital between about 1300 BCE and the end of the Shang dynasty in 1021 BCE. During these years, a succession of Shang rulers turned the city into China's political, economic, military, and cultural center. Yin's excavated ruins have earned what is left of the city a designation as a UNESCO World Heritage site. It spanned an area of close to 100 acres that was surrounded by a wall and a larger area of several square miles that contained most of the city's population of over 100,000 inhabitants. Yin contained (within its walled precincts) a walled palace, 200 residences (mostly for upper-class officials), and thousands of tombs. Between 772 and 480 BCE, according to one estimate, seventy-eight additional cities arose in China's north. Urbanization also took place in east-central China along the Yangtze River, farther south in coastal regions, and on Taiwan. As a result, around 500 BCE, China already had four to six cities with populations in excess of 100,000 inhabitants. So many cities of such size were not to be found in any other region of the world at the time.

Across the Atlantic Ocean, in the middle and northern parts of Latin America, cities may have been founded by Olmecs and Mayans as early as the seventh century BCE. By 600 BCE, there were also cities in the Andean region. Tiwanaku, now a UNESCO World Heritage site, may have been one of them, although it did not become prominent until long thereafter.

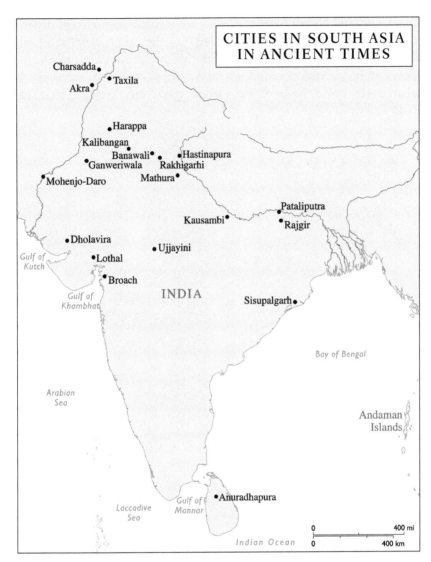

**CITIES IN SOUTH ASIA
IN ANCIENT TIMES**

Charsadda
Taxila
Akra
Harappa
Kalibangan
Banawali
Ganweriwala
Rakhigarhi
Hastinapura
Mohenjo-Daro
Mathura
Pataliputra
Kausambi
Rajgir
Dholavira
Gulf of
Kutch
Lothal
Ujjayini
Broach
Gulf of
Khambhat
INDIA
Sisupalgarh
Bay of Bengal
Arabian
Sea
Andaman
Islands
Laccadive
Sea
Gulf of
Mannar
Anuradhapura
Indian Ocean

0   400 mi
0   400 km

*Widespread urbanization took place in South Asia, in what is now India
and Pakistan, slightly later than in the Middle East. The Indus Valley was a
major center of urban development, which became particularly apparent in
Mohenjo-Daro and Harappa.* Based on a map by Niko Lipsanen.

Around the middle of the first millennium BCE, urban growth
varied widely from one part of the world to another. In most regions,
cities were still rare phenomena. In Australia, northern Asia,
northern Europe, Africa south of the Sahara Desert, and most of

both South and North America, cities were either nonexistent or very few in number and very small in size. On the other hand, from the Mediterranean to Southwest Asia, South Asia, China, and, albeit to a lesser extent, in Mexico and Central America, numerous networks of urban centers laid the basis for a great age of city-building that was about to begin.

CHAPTER 2

Great Cities, 500 BCE–300 CE

The second half of the first millennium BCE and several centuries thereafter witnessed the flowering of a vibrant urban civilization on the shores of the Mediterranean Sea, many traces of which are still visited and inspected not only by archaeologists and historians but also by hordes of admiring tourists. On a scale much vaster than anything undertaken by the Phoenicians before them, enterprising and expansive Greeks and Romans carried out an impressive program of city-building. They established hundreds of urban settlements along the coast of North Africa, as well as in the western parts of present-day Turkey and Europe. Ensconced within networks of cities that linked them to large numbers of other places over which they exercised a high degree of influence and control, Athens (a city-state) and Rome (the capital of an empire) emerged as the leading urban centers in the Mediterranean area in classical antiquity.

Athens had many more inhabitants than any of the other Greek cities (e.g., Corinth and Sparta). If one counts both the city itself and the surrounding area governed by Athens (known as Attica), its population exceeded 200,000. Its size certainly contributed to its preeminence in relation to its neighbors, but size is not what deserves the most attention. Although Athenians, unlike citizens of other Greek city-states, did not stand out as founders of colonies far from home, their city was distinguished as an extraordinarily dynamic center of urban life. As such, it exercised a considerable influence over other cities in its region during the fifth century BCE and, by example, over people who lived elsewhere in later centuries. Particularly during the fifth century, a "golden age" in the Athenian past, the city experienced developments and displayed qualities that have led scholars to call it a cradle if not *the* cradle of Western civilization.

Athenian inventiveness manifested itself in architecture, political institutions, literature, and philosophy. The stage for Athenian greatness was set by a combination of domestic and foreign events. In the first place, the rule of the tyrant Peisistratus and his sons gave way in 508 BCE under the leadership of the Athenian Cleisthenes to a relatively democratic form of government. The leading Athenian statesman Pericles expressed pride in Athens for its political and civic excellence in a 431 BCE funeral oration for the war dead in a conflict with Sparta. The Athenian historian Thucydides, writing not long after the speech was given, reconstructed what he thought Pericles had said:

> Our constitution does not copy the laws of neighboring states; we are rather a pattern to others than imitators ourselves. Its administration favors the many instead of the few; this is why it is called a democracy. If we look to the laws, they afford equal justice to all in their private differences; if to social standing, advancement in public life falls to reputation for capacity, class considerations not being allowed to interfere with merit; nor again does poverty bar the way, if a man is able to serve the state, he is not hindered by the obscurity of his condition.

According to Thucydides, Pericles went on to assert: "We Athenians are able to judge at all events if we cannot originate, and instead of looking on discussion as a stumbling-block in the way of action, we think it an indispensable preliminary to any wise action at all." In Pericles's view, a city that was marked by such a high degree of equality and liberty as was evident in Athens richly deserved the affection of its citizens, which he eloquently urged his listeners to make manifest.[1]

Athens was not what we regard today as a democracy. Women played no part in governmental processes, and roughly one-third of the population consisted of slaves, whose voices were also excluded from discussions of public affairs. Nonetheless, among free men, legal equality and equal rights to vote in citizens' assemblies and hold public office prevailed, giving Athenians the right to claim that they had invented the idea and the practice of popular sovereignty.

Athens's rise to its fifth-century apogee was also furthered by the outcome and aftermath of its successful leadership of the Greeks in earlier wars. They had come together in order to defend themselves against mighty armies and fleets from Persia, whose commanders sought to expand the Persian Empire at Greek expense. In several big battles on land and on water between 490 and 479 BCE, Persian forces were defeated, and the threat posed by non-Greeks to Greek independence was averted. As a result of the leading role it had played in the conflict,

Athens emerged with its power and prestige in the region greatly enhanced, and its primacy among the Greek city-states remained unquestioned for several decades.

The image of Athens was improved not only by its reputation for self-government and its military virtues, but also by its architecture and other cultural attainments. Despite the fact that Athenians and their allies had held the Persians at bay, their city had suffered a good deal of physical devastation. But this too contributed to Athens' rise, inasmuch as it led to the launching of a massive program of reconstruction. Under Pericles's leadership, during a period of only a few decades, numerous impressive structures were completed. Private squalor prevailed in overcrowded residential areas, but there was a great deal of public opulence and magnificence. Five centuries later, the Greek historian Plutarch described the construction this way: "As then the works grew up, no less stately in size than exquisite in form . . . yet the most wonderful thing was the rapidity of their execution. Undertakings, any one of which might singly have required . . . for their completion, several successions and ages of men, were every one of them accomplished in the height and prime of one man's political service."[2] Focused on the erection of buildings that served a variety of public purposes, this project gave visible expression to the spirit of civic-mindedness that animated and was nourished by free men's involvement as citizens in public affairs. In and around an outdoor civic center known as the agora, men gathered to participate in governmental business, buy and sell goods, engage in athletic events, attend theatrical performances, and worship in temples.

Greek architecture reached its zenith above the agora on a rocky plateau known as the Acropolis. After passing through the Propylaea, a monumental gate, one came to a temple called the Erectheum, which was dedicated to an early Athenian hero, and finally to the Parthenon, also a temple and the single most famous and admired building to be constructed during the years of classical antiquity. With its forty-six Doric columns that surrounded the inner space and its stately statues, produced under the direction of the sculptor Phidias, that were ensconced between them and the building's roof, the aesthetically exquisite Parthenon embodied devotion not only to the goddess Athene but also to the city she symbolized. The frieze's depictions celebrated the city and the unity of its citizens.

In drama and philosophy, Greek thinkers examined the human condition. Many plays were publicly performed. The greatest of the fifth-century Greek playwrights were Aeschylus, Sophocles, and

The Parthenon, with its friezes by the sculptor Phidias, was the foremost of several impressive civic buildings that were constructed on the Acropolis in Athens during the fifth century BCE. *Religious ceremonies that took place in these buildings paid tribute to Greek gods but also to the city itself as a community of citizens.* Royal Ontario Museum, Toronto, accession number 956.118.

Euripides. In tragedies written in poetry, such as the trilogy known as the *Oresteia* (by Aeschylus), *Oedipus the King* and *Antigone* (by Sophocles), and *The Medea* (by Euripides), these authors raised profound issues having to do with familial conflicts, conflicts between religious and moral obligations, and conflicts regarding the rule of law. How to resolve such conflicts in the interests of justice was the problem that these dramatists addressed. Sophocles in particular sought to show how the possession of power could undermine one's sense of moral responsibility (as in the case of King Creon in *Antigone*). There was also a rich outpouring of theatrical comedies, most notably written by Aristophanes. He openly pilloried a wide range of targets, among them the Greeks' gods, as well as statesmen like Pericles, other politicians and bureaucrats, military men, businessmen, and intellectuals. A high degree of freedom of speech made it possible for him and others to criticize many men and practices, such as imperialism, war-profiteering, and the pursuit of power by unscrupulous politicians, thus calling into question unattractive aspects of the city.

Philosophy also flourished, particularly as embodied in the person of Socrates. Professing his own ignorance, he sought to enlighten others by relentlessly asking them to reflect on how they knew what they thought they knew. Known as "the gadfly of Athens," he was eventually sentenced to death for religious heresies and for "corrupting" Athenian youth with his questioning, but his intellectual legacy was kept alive by his pupil Plato.

Following the outbreak of the war that began in 431 BCE between Athens and Sparta, which was supported by other Greek city-states whose rulers feared the growth of Athenian power in the region, the Athenian democracy suffered a series of severe blows. These culminated in Athenian defeat in 404 BCE. At this time, under Spartan dictates, Athens was required to tear down a long wall that protected the road that led to its port area and to accept an oligarchic government that was known as "the thirty tyrants." Athens never regained its former importance. In 338 BCE, Athens experienced another defeat, this time at the hands of Philip II, who was the ruler of the Greek kingdom of Macedon. Athens now came under foreign rule (becoming part of the Roman Empire in 146 BCE). The fourth century nonetheless witnessed a continuing output of a high order in the areas of literature and philosophy. The comic poet Aristophanes continued to write works for the stage that contained heavy doses of political and social satire up until his death in 388 BCE. Thereafter, Plato and his pupil Aristotle gained great and lasting fame and influence as both philosophers and educators, Aristotle having served as a teacher not only in Athens but also in neighboring Macedonia as a tutor to King Philip's son Alexander.

Alexander achieved great renown as a territorial conqueror whose imperial realm reached from Greece and Egypt all the way to northern India within only a few years. In this area, he established seventy cities, largely for the purpose of strengthening his grip on the lands he had acquired. These and other cities flourished in the eastern Mediterranean during and after the fourth century BCE (e.g., Pergamon and Antioch). They also served as nodal points for the spread of Greek (or Hellenic) influences to non-Greeks long after Alexander's early death and the dissolution of the empire he had built. Among the many cities he named after himself, Alexandria (founded in 332 BCE as a port city in northern Egypt) shined as the leader of urban life in the Western world. With a population of between 200,000 and 500,000 inhabitants in ancient times, Alexandria exceeded Rome in size, wealth, and splendor between the third and first centuries BCE. It served as the capital of a kingdom ruled by the Greek Ptolemies (including the Empress Cleopatra) until the area was conquered by the Romans in 30 BCE.

Laid out according to Alexander's instructions by the Greek city planner Dinocrates of Rhodes in a grid pattern, the city extended about four miles from east to west and was surrounded by a wall that was supposedly nine miles in length. Within or adjacent to this area, a multitude of imposing structures bore witness not only to the city's commercial wealth (much of it based on the export of ivory, ebony, spices, and grain), but also to the ambitions of its Ptolemaic rulers. They used monumental architecture as a means of both demonstrating and enhancing their dynastic power. The Greek geographer Strabo, writing between 7 and 18 CE, praised their achievements:

> The city is full of public and sacred buildings, but the most beautiful of them is the Gymnasium, which has porticoes more than a stadium [200 yards] in length. And in the middle [of the city] there are both the court of justice and the groves. . . . And the city contains most beautiful public precincts and also the royal palaces, which constitute one-fourth or even one-third of the whole circuit of the city. . . . The Museum is also part of the royal palaces; it has a public walk, an exedra with seats [a semicircular outside area intended for conversation], and a large house in which there is the common room of the scholars who are fellows of the Museum.[3]

The Ptolemies constructed a gigantic lighthouse several hundred feet in height. Known as one of the Seven Wonders of the Ancient World, it was erected about 280 BCE on the island of Pharos at the point of entry to the great port. A profusion of other buildings proclaimed Alexandrian prosperity and eminence, especially along a magnificent thoroughfare named Canopus Street.

Like Athens, Alexandria enjoyed preeminence among cities not only because of its buildings but also—and more significantly—because of what they contained. The museum praised by Strabo included what was reputed to be the largest library in the world. Consisting of some 700,000 works on papyrus rolls that were either written in or translated into Greek, the library served as a research center. Scholars came here from within the city and elsewhere in Egypt and also from many other countries in order to acquire and share knowledge. They thus entered into a community that was marked by ethnic, cultural, and religious diversity, which greatly stimulated intellectual life. Eratosthenes, who became the chief librarian in 236 BCE, made calculations on the basis of travelers' reports that enabled him to draw the first map of the known world, which showed the continents of Europe, Africa, and Asia.

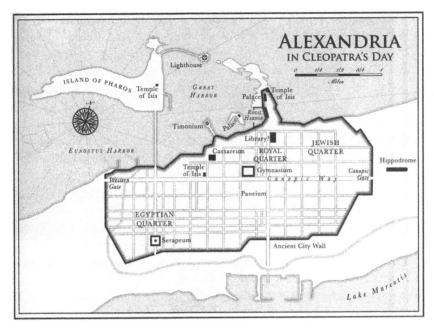

Medical researchers, who engaged in vivisection, as well as dissection of corpses, described parts of the brain, the valves of the heart, and the links between veins and arteries. Other scholars who congregated in Alexandria translated the Old Testament into Greek, and thus produced a text that was to become an essential part of the foundation for Christianity. In all these ways and in many others, Alexandria richly deserved its reputation as the cultural capital of the Hellenistic world.

When the kingdom of the Ptolemies, together with its capital Alexandria, lost its independence, it was absorbed into an empire the core of which had been established more than half a millennium earlier. What was to become the empire's mighty capital, the city of Rome, dated back to around the middle of the eighth century BCE. Having brought most of Italy and much of its territory to the north inhabited by the Etruscans beneath its sway by around 270 BCE, Rome grew steadily in size. By 150 BCE, it numbered at least 300,000 inhabitants.

The city reached its demographic height during the second century CE. At that time, its population amounted to at least 700,000 inhabitants and perhaps as many as 1.2 million. It was the first giant city in world history—a city far superior numerically (and in other ways as well) to any other city that had previously existed. Originally ruled by kings, Rome, like Athens, became a republic in about 500 BCE. Unlike the Athenian republic, however, the Roman republic was dominated by land-owning aristocrats who controlled the Roman senate. Nonetheless, non-aristocrats known as plebeians were also represented, and in 287 BCE, these men gained additional power.

In later centuries, Roman republicanism lost its earlier vitality as slave revolts and greed among members of the upper classes undermined stability. Eventually, the republic gave way to a political system in which supreme power was held by hereditary emperors, the first of whom, Caesar Augustus, sat on the imperial throne between 27 BCE and 14 CE. The decline of the old regime and the emergence of a new one were accompanied and followed by steady growth in the size of the territory over which Rome's governors ruled, which reached its height early in the second century CE. At this time, the Roman Empire extended almost all the way around the Mediterranean and also to the north, including Spain, Gaul (now France), and most of Britain. As the empire expanded, its capital became not only vastly more populous but also much more affluent, in large part because it could take huge amounts of resources from subject peoples.

Growing as it did over a period of many centuries, Rome, unlike Alexandria, did not reflect the unifying vision of a master planner. For a long time, its streets were narrow and noisy; its multistory residences were severely overcrowded; and the city's inhabitants were subjected to periodic outbreaks of typhoid, typhus, and cholera. But, like Athens and Alexandria, Rome benefited from an architectural tradition that bore witness to an abiding belief in the value of public buildings and services, even though the latter were inadequate in view of the city's growing size and density.

Already during the republican period, governmental officials took responsibility, either at public expense or their own, for the construction of public facilities. Early in the second century BCE, public halls (basilicas) were erected in a central meeting place known as the forum. Early in the following century, a public archive (the Tabularium) appeared in the same area. Later, successful generals used parts of their spoils for similar purposes. Pompey, a civilian official after serving as a general, erected Rome's first permanent stone theater with profits reaped from military campaigns. Similarly, Julius Caesar initiated the construction of yet another basilica in the forum, which served as a sheltered space in which to conduct business during bad weather. Meanwhile, in the same area, the Curia had been built as a meeting place for the Senate, and three temples had also been constructed.

The greatest surge in the construction of new buildings took place during the reign of and at the behest of Caesar Augustus, who is said to have boasted: "I left Rome a city of marble, though I found her a city of bricks."[4] The chronicler Suetonius, writing over a century after Augustus's death, testified to his lasting accomplishments:

> As for public safety, he provided against human disasters so far as human foresight could do so. He constructed a very large number of public buildings. . . . He also frequently urged other leading public men to embellish the city by constructing new public monuments or restoring old ones, according to their means. . . . Against fires, he organized water-companies and firemen; against flood he cleared and scoured the channel of the Tiber. . . . He restored ruined or burned temples and enriched them with the most princely gifts.[5]

Most of the projects Augustus initiated were concentrated on two central hills (the Capitoline and the Palatine) and in the area around the forum. In these places, there were a triumphal arch that celebrated recent military victories, a mausoleum for Augustus and his family, a theater, a new forum, which he named after himself, and dozens of new temples. In addition to commissioning new buildings, he also took important steps to keep the aqueducts that brought water into the city in good repair. In accordance with prevailing taste, many of these structures emulated Greek styles, particularly the ornamental Corinthian style. In Augustus's view, the capital of the world's greatest empire required a public face that would be commensurate with the empire's high status. Augustus sought by means of his building projects not only to polish the image of his capital but also enhance his own reputation. But there can be no denying the extent of his achievement in refurbishing his city physically. One can easily see how Augustan building projects in Rome, as well as expansion outside of it, must have helped to foster the tributes bestowed on Augustus by writers such as the historian Livy and the poet Virgil, both of whom were active during his reign. The growth of Rome's power was a central part of this narrative, but the sense of power was increasingly buttressed by pride in its splendid buildings.

One of Augustus's least admired successors, the Emperor Nero, dedicated vast resources after a disastrous fire that occurred in 64 CE to construction of an enormous and extraordinarily opulent palace. Suetonius described Nero's new residence with evident distaste:

> Of its dimensions and furniture, it may be sufficient to say this much: the porch was so high that there stood in it a colossal statue of himself a hundred and twenty feet in height. . . . In other parts it was entirely overlaid with gold, and adorned with jewels and mother of pearl. The supper rooms were vaulted, and compartments of the ceilings, inlaid with ivory, were made to revolve, and scatter flowers. . . . Upon the dedication of this magnificent house after it was finished, all he said in approval of it was "that he now had a dwelling fit for a man."[6]

In addition, however, Nero promoted improvements that were designed to benefit the city as a whole, imposing a city plan on Rome for the first time. Heights of houses were limited, fireproof building materials were required, minimum widths for streets were decreed, and street layouts were prescribed.

In later years, other architectural projects, while quite grand in scale, pointed away from obvious self-glorification toward a continuation of long-standing traditions of public utility—or at least the idea that public space was an essential ingredient of a good city. Like Augustus, subsequent emperors sought to enhance their reputations as city builders. They constructed or reconstructed temples (the most notable among them being the Pantheon, first built in 27 BCE and rebuilt between 115 and 124 CE), theaters, circuses, bathhouses, and other places in which they and their subjects could gather for leisure-time activities.

Among these places, the Circus Maximus (which could hold 150,000 spectators) and the Colosseum (which held up to 50,000), both finished early in the second century, stood out as major venues for Roman entertainments. Many of the events that occurred in these places, with their emphasis on mass spectacles, were often quite violent (particularly the gladiatorial combats that occurred in the Colosseum, although the chariot races in the Circus Maximus were also fierce). The masses were not only brutalized but also pacified, inasmuch as amusement (together with handouts of food, whence the phrase "bread and circuses") compensated them for subjugation. Nonetheless, in such spaces, ordinary people gained a sense of themselves as members of an urban community that transcended the unwholesome neighborhoods in which many of them lived.

More obviously useful purposes were served by other massive structures. Built at a time when indoor plumbing was seldom to be

Constructed toward the end of the first century CE, the Colosseum was an elliptical amphitheater near the center of Rome. It could accommodate up to 80,000 spectators who watched many violent entertainments, including struggles to the death between gladiators and the feeding of Christians to lions.
© Vanni Archive/Art Resource, NY, ART317601.

found, the baths of Caracalla (constructed early in the third century) and other baths were valuable from both a recreational and a hygienic standpoint. The Romans also excelled at improving the quality of urban life by making their city cleaner and healthier, and they undertook other initiatives that reflected advanced technological know-how as well. Ample supplies of water for drinking and for carrying away human and animal waste products were essential in a city of Rome's size and density, and the Romans worked hard to ensure their availability. Starting with a conduit constructed in the fourth century BCE that brought water underground from springs over six miles away, the Romans built up a vast network of waterways, including both canals and aqueducts that carried water over valleys. By the fourth century CE, these structures brought over 200 million gallons of water per day from distant mountains. The water was stored in reservoirs and was pumped from them not only to the houses of the rich but also to public fountains, as well as bathhouses.

Rome similarly benefited from an extensive network of sewers known as the cloaca maxima. Dating back to the sixth century BCE, the sewers reached their peak of capacity and efficiency in the first century CE. The system was by no means universal; most Romans relied on outhouse toilets, and much sewage continued to flow in open channels along city streets. Still, as late as the 1840s, public health reformers in Britain regarded parts of the system as superior to anything yet operational in their country.

The Romans were also quite advanced with regard to infrastructure that supported transportation. In large measure for military reasons, they constructed the most extensive network of roads during ancient times anywhere in Eurasia. The first one connected Rome with Capua, near Naples, in 312 BCE. In later centuries, Romans built 50,000 additional miles of roads, which (together with ships) helped to connect their capital with distant provinces. Four feet thick and consisting of five layers of sand, stones, and clay or cement, many of these roads are still in use today.

Like the Greeks before them, the Romans founded numerous cities in areas far away from their home base. Although many of these cities, such as Ostia (which arose as a port for Rome itself where the Tiber River ran into the Mediterranean) and Pompeii, were located in Italy, numerous others were located much farther afield. Not counting cities in Italy, there were probably more than 350 cities with populations of more than 5,000 in the empire at its height that had been either founded or fostered by the Romans. The empire contained more than 140 cities on the Iberian peninsula (e.g., Cordoba), at least 130 in Gaul (e.g., Lyon and Trier), and 47 in Britain (e.g., London), as well as several cities in northern Africa to the west of Alexandria. Wherever they established or governed urban communities, Roman city builders displayed the same practical concerns that were so clearly evident in their management of the city of Rome itself. Most of the cities in the empire enjoyed, like Rome, high levels of public works. They had abundant supplies of water, large baths, well-designed systems of drainage, splendid temples and theaters, and many other public buildings that were large and imposing.

Although we are not nearly as well informed about the history of individual cities elsewhere during the ancient period as we are about cities around the Mediterranean, large urban settlements arose and thrived far outside the orbits of Greece and Rome. Outside of northern Africa, significant cities arose in what is now Ethiopia after about 100 CE in the kingdom of Aksum, where a city by that name became the kingdom's capital.

Megasthenes, a Greek ambassador stationed in the South Asian capital of Pataliputra between 304 and 299, regarded that city as one of the greatest in the world. His writing has been lost, but according to summaries of it, he asserted (with what was probably a good deal of exaggeration) that the city was 9.5 miles long and a mile and a half broad; that it was protected by a moat sixty feet deep and 600 feet wide; and that it was further protected by a massive timber palisade punctuated by sixty-four gates and 570 towers. Attached to the royal residence was a good-sized park, "in which were tame peacocks and pheasants. . . . There were [also] shady groves and trees set in clumps and branches woven together by some special cunning of horticulture."[7]

Pataliputra represented a new era of city building in what is now India after a long period of urban stagnation that had followed the collapse of cities in the Indus Valley. From the middle to late part of the first millennium BCE well into the first millennium CE, numerous cities developed in South Asia, including a multitude of administrative centers—regional capitals and imperial ones, such as Pataliputra. The capital of the Mauryan Empire in north-central India, it was constructed starting in 490 BCE at the confluence of two rivers, the Ganges and the Son.

Pataliputra reached its height during the rule of Ashoka the Great in the third century BCE. Its population then may have been as high as 350,000, which would have made it as large as, if not larger than, Rome. During his reign, Ashoka strengthened his capital's walls, constructed within them a magnificent palace in which there was an immense hall that covered a square 250 feet on each side, and sponsored the construction of several Buddhist monasteries.

Like other great cities at the time, Pataliputra stood out as a center of political power, but it was also a center of trade and commerce, forging economic links with both China and the Roman Empire, and a cultural center. Overall, Mauryan culture was heavily religious, reflecting the city's role as a center of Buddhism. The city was, however, also noted as a center of literature and scholarship, attracting secular intellectuals, as well as monks and merchants. The most prominent of these men, named Chanakya, who was born around 370 BCE, produced pioneering works in the areas of economics and political science, earning later references to him as "the Indian Machiavelli."

Having constructed a dense urban network of commercial and administrative centers, inhabitants of China could boast by the later years of the Zhou dynasty (around 500 BCE) of perhaps as many as half a dozen cities with populations of 100,000 or more, and their energetic urban construction persisted thereafter. A period known as the Warring States (475–221 BCE) witnessed unprecedented city-building. Every ruler of a state had a capital. Protective walls surrounded most capitals and other cities as well. In capitals, walled palaces constituted additionally protected areas, and they often occupied the center of the city, thus gaining in symbolic significance. The development of cities reached an early peak during the Han dynasty (202 BCE to 220 CE), a period marked by a relatively high degree of internal peace, territorial expansion, and artistic achievement. The two greatest of the Han cities were both capitals: Chang'an and Luoyang. Palaces, mausoleums, and ritual architecture marked these settlements. Luoyang became particularly noteworthy for its hundreds of Buddhist and Daoist temples and monasteries, which increasingly stood alongside Confucian temples and temples dedicated to local gods. Visitors to the Longmen Grottoes, located near Luoyang, can still see thousands of statues of Buddha and his disciples, produced starting in the late fifth century. Markets also became more widely evident. Chang'an had a western market that covered 250,000 square meters and an eastern market that was twice as big. A contemporary observer of the Chang'an markets, Ban Mengjian, authored a "Western Capital Rhapsody" in which he celebrated "shopgirls [who] were dressed more lavishly than ladies" and wrote:

> The pedlars, shopkeepers, and common people
> Male and female vendors, selling cheap,
> Sold good quality mixed with the shoddy,
> Dazzling the eyes of the country bumpkins.
> Why exert oneself in performing labor,
> When devious earnings were so plentiful?

These Chinese could take pride in having acquired commercial skills that stood them in good stead in their relations with gullible visitors to their city from rural areas.[8]

Meanwhile, halfway around the world, cities were also developing in Mexico and in adjoining Guatemala. In a marshy area known as the Valley of Mexico, around 350 BCE, Cuicuilco and Teotihuacan comprised at least 2,500 acres and had populations of 20,000 or more inhabitants. To their south, in the Yucatán, Mayan cities grew up around ceremonial centers such as El Mirador, which became the Mayan capital, and Tikal. El Mirador flourished approximately between the middle of the first millennium BCE and the early part of the first millennium CE, when it had a population of between 40,000 and 80,000. At that time, Tikal was smaller, but it was growing, and during the eighth and ninth centuries, when Mayan civilization reached its apogee, its population stood at well over 100,000.

Abandoned many centuries ago, the sites of these cities have been well excavated, and what is left of the structures the Mayans built offers eloquent evidence of a high degree of urban energy. Located on hilly land above surrounding swamps, the remains of Tikal include nine groups of courtyards and plazas connected by bridges and causeways. Temples located in a central area that covers about 500 acres rise above the courtyards and plazas, the most imposing of these structures being a temple that reaches a height of 229 feet. Devoid though they are of inhabitants, remnants of Tikal survive as powerful reminders of urban developments of great magnitude.

CHAPTER 3

Decline and Development, 300–1500

Between the early fourth and the early ninth centuries, European cities declined or, at best, grew very slowly in comparison with what had taken place in earlier centuries. Although the so-called Dark Ages that constituted the first part of the Middle Ages were not as uncongenial to life in cities as that name suggests, this period stands out on the whole in the West as one of urban retrogression. Even a century before the formal end of the Roman Empire in the West in 476, decline was increasingly apparent. Invasions by hordes of Germanic tribes and other "barbarians" (e.g., Visigoths, Vandals, Huns, and Ostrogoths) whose home bases lay to the north and east severely disrupted trade and commerce and caused a general sense of insecurity. Municipal authorities constructed walls to protect their precincts and inhabitants from raids and destruction by outsiders. But they did so to little avail, and many cities were sacked. Rome was one of them, suffering in 410 at the hands of Alaric, king of the Visigoths.

As Saint Jerome wrote not long after this assault, "Rome had been besieged and its citizens had been forced to buy their lives with gold. Then thus despoiled they had been besieged again so as to lose not their substance only but their lives. My voice sticks in my throat; and, as I dictate, sobs choke my utterance. The City which had taken the whole world was itself taken; nay more famine was beforehand with the sword and but few citizens were left to be made captives."[1] Romans fled to the countryside for safety. They took up residence in rural hamlets, castles, or monasteries. The rise of Christianity, with its emphasis on otherworldliness, also tended to promote urban decline, inasmuch as it worked to discourage involvement in the secular life of municipalities. To be sure, bishoprics were centered in urban areas. The Christian Church had taken over the urban grid established by the Romans, and in this sense, churchmen helped to maintain cities that had been founded by pagans. But writings by Christian theologians exuded none of the civic pride articulated by classical authors. Indeed, Saint Augustine, in an enormously influential work written in 410 titled *The City of God*, excoriated Rome as the archetypal "city of man" whose history he invoked as proof of human frailty and sin.

Rome itself, which boasted a population of around a million in the second century, had only about 50,000 inhabitants around 700, a number that was to fall to around 35,000 by the start of the eleventh century. Elsewhere in Italy, the cities of Cremona and Padua were destroyed, roads were abandoned, and sewage systems collapsed. In Gaul (France), many people abandoned urban centers. Consequently, places such as Tours and Lyon retained only small portions of their earlier populations and functions. In Britain, only a few of what had formerly functioned as major urban centers—London, Lincoln, Canterbury, York, and Chester—continued to be inhabited to any significant degree. In Europe as a whole (excluding Russia), the overall population living in settlements that numbered 2,000 or more inhabitants fell by about 40 percent between 200 and 500 CE and at least 20 percent in the next 200 to 250 years.

Urban vigor shifted to Europe's east. The Roman Emperor Constantine selected the site of a Greek village known as Byzantion for a new capital. Established between 324 and 330, Constantinople was located in the far western part of what is now Turkey next to a body of water (the Bosporus Straits) that forms part of the channel from the Black Sea to the Mediterranean. It flourished as one of the world's largest cities for many centuries, replacing Rome as the major Mediterranean metropolis. It was far and away the leading city in what came to be known, following the fall of the Roman Empire's western half in 476, as the Byzantine Empire—an empire that lasted for almost 1,000 years. With a population of some 250,000 to 350,000 in 390, the city fluctuated from about 450 to 1070 between 400,000 and 600,000 inhabitants. During this period, its population was at least ten times that of any other city in the Byzantine Empire and at least six times the size of any other city in Christian Europe, the next biggest being Palermo with a population of about 75,000 in 1000.

Constantinople's preeminence resulted not only from its political status as an imperial capital but also from the wealth it garnered via international commerce. Because it was on the major trading routes that ran from east to west between Europe and Asia and from north to south between the Black Sea and areas along the shore of the eastern part of the Mediterranean, Constantinople was at the heart of a far-flung network of trading partners. Its harbor and streets were heavily populated by international merchants who came from many lands. The presence of Russians, West Europeans, and Arabs, some of whom brought wares from as far as India and China, gave the city a markedly cosmopolitan quality and added greatly to its material prosperity.

The fruits of commerce enabled the empire's rulers—most notably, in addition to Constantine, his fifth- and sixth-century successors, Theodosius II and Justinian—to create a legacy of building that elicited great admiration from natives and foreigners alike. Constantine himself laid out much of the basic plan of the city. He provided for a major forum that was to serve as the city's commercial center, as well as a spacious palace and a hippodrome that functioned as an equivalent of the Circus Maximus in Rome. Walls built under Theodosius's direction between 413 and 447 solidified the city's defensive position, constituting another impressive feature of the urban landscape.

But the most important of the city's many imposing structures were its churches, where churchmen sought to inculcate Christians' religious obligations to obey their emperors. Among these buildings, one stands out above all the others: the Hagia Sophia (Holy Wisdom). Not long after it was finished in 537, the Byzantine historian Procopius of Caesarea wrote that it was "distinguished by indescribable beauty, excelling both in its size, and in the harmony of its measures, having no part excessive and none deficient; being more magnificent than ordinary buildings, and much more elegant than those which are not of so just a proportion. The church was singularly full of light and sunshine; you would declare that the place is not lighted by the sun from without, but that the rays are produced within itself, such an abundance of light is poured into this church."[2]

Many centuries later, a Frenchman recounted the astonishment of Crusaders from Western Europe as they approached the city in 1204 in order to attack it. "Indeed you should know," he wrote, "that they gazed well at Constantinople, those who had never seen it; for they could not believe that there could be in all the world a city so rich, when they saw those tall ramparts and the mighty towers with which it was shut all around, and those rich palaces and those tall churches, of which there were so many that nobody could believe their eyes, had they not seen it, and the length and breadth of the city which was sovereign among all others."[3]

These men proceeded to sack the city they were said to admire, thereby accelerating a process of urban decline that had already been

The Hagia Sophia was completed in 537 under the direction of Emperor Justinian as a Christian church. It is the supreme example of Byzantine art and one of the foremost examples of religious architecture anywhere in the world. The slender minarets were added when the building was turned into a mosque following the Ottoman Turks' 1453 takeover of the city. Courtesy of Arild Vågen/Wikimedia Commons/CC-BY-SA-3.0

apparent since the city had reached its zenith late in the eleventh century. After a western occupation that lasted until 1261, a Greek emperor, Michael VIII Palaeologus, ended the reign of the Latin emperors who had been imposed by the Crusaders. But the city of which he took possession had suffered and continued to suffer a great loss of population, which fell, by the mid–fifteenth century, to 40,000–50,000 inhabitants. Partly as a result of this loss, it was unable to withstand subsequent assaults by Ottoman Turks. Continuing a push to the west that had begun several centuries earlier, these Muslims took control for good in 1453, thus bringing the Byzantine Empire to a definitive end. (Increasingly, it was henceforth referred to as Istanbul, although its name was not changed officially until the 1920s.)

The men who conquered Constantinople in the mid–fifteenth century were heirs to a tradition of Muslim expansionism that dated back to the seventh century, when the Arab prophet Muhammad founded the religion that came to be known as Islam. He had aimed to spread the new faith far and wide, not only by evangelizing but also by politically controlling large areas. Consequently, around 750, Muslims held sway over large parts of Southwest Asia, northern Africa, and the Iberian Peninsula. As they extended and tightened both their religious and political grip, Muslims turned away from a nomadic way of life and toward cities, such as Damascus, Jerusalem, Alexandria, Tripoli, Seville, and Cordoba (with a population at the start of the eleventh century of perhaps 400,000 to 500,000 inhabitants and 3,000 mosques). Caliphs (royal rulers) also established a smaller number of new cities, enhancing their power—administratively and symbolically—via the construction of impressive capitals.

Among such cities, none was more imposing or noteworthy than Baghdad. By the mid–eleventh century, teacher and preacher Al-Khatib al-Baghdadi wrote in a history of Baghdad:

> In the entire world, there has not been a city which could compare with Baghdad in size or splendor, or in the number of scholars and great personalities. The distinction of the notables and general populace serves to distinguish Baghdad from the other cities, as does the vastness of its districts, the extent of its borders, and the great number of residences and palaces. Consider the numerous roads, thoroughfares, and localities, the markets and streets, the lanes, mosques and bathhouses, and the high roads and shops—all of these distinguish the city from all others. . . . The very great population also distinguishes it from all other cities.[4]

Large numbers of impressive "personalities" as well as built structures both private and public bore witness in the author's eyes to an ascendancy that had begun several centuries earlier.

Baghdad started to arise as a new city in 762 at the behest of the Abbasid Caliph Al-Mansur, and what he had had in mind was largely finished by 765. As a new foundation, it evinced a degree of planning and regularity that distinguished it from most other cities in the Islamic world. The city was laid out in the form of a circle. At the center was the royal palace, capped by an immense green dome that reached 160 feet into the air. Next to it stood a huge mosque. A high-walled open ring separated the palace and the mosque from the rest of the city. A moat surrounded the wall, which was pierced by four fortified gates. A beneficiary, like Constantinople, of its strategic position along the trade route between Europe and Southwest Asia and East Asia, as well as of its status as a capital, Baghdad grew quite rapidly. By 800, it probably had at least 400,000 inhabitants. By 850, it was the largest city in the world, and by 930, it had a population on the order of one million.

As Baghdad grew, it played an increasingly significant role in Muslim intellectual life, reaching its peak demographically and culturally during the late-eighth- and early-ninth-century reigns of Caliph Harun al-Rashid and his son Mamun. Cosmopolitan mixtures of Persians, Turks, Arabs, Muslims, Christians, Jews, and Zoroastrians, combined with ambitious rulers, made Baghdad a vital center of science and learning. Determined to make Baghdad the intellectual, as well as the political, capital of their empire, they encouraged the translation of many Greek manuscripts obtained from Constantinople into Arabic, founded an astronomical observatory, and supported medical research. They also supported philosophers who sought to synthesize Muslim philosophy with the teachings of Aristotle.

The city was attacked and sacked in 1258 by Mongols, who destroyed nearly all its splendor. It revived, but it was captured again by the Mongol conqueror Tamerlane in 1400 and then by the Persians in 1524, before being absorbed into the Ottoman Empire in 1524. During its decline, in 1437, the Egyptian historian Al-Maqrisi wrote, "Baghdad is in ruin; there are no more mosques, believers, call to prayer or market. Most of the pine trees have dried up; most of the channels are blocked. It can no longer be called a city."[5] Such was the perceived condition of what for centuries had been one of the largest and most remarkable cities in the world.

From Southwest Asia, the fabled international network known as the Silk Road stretched thousands of miles to East Asia, the place of origin of silk and other luxury goods. In imperial China, robust networks of cities performed as economic centers of distribution. Some were located along rivers that permitted easy access to the ocean, while others, located farther inland, functioned as either regional market towns or anchors of the Silk Road. But the dominant places in the Chinese urban network were administrative centers. From the trunks of great imperial capitals branched regional and provincial capitals, which in turn forked into 2,000 county capitals around the year 1000.

One of the most extraordinary of these imperial capitals was Chang'an (now Xian), which reached its height near China's geographic center at approximately the same time as Baghdad attained its peak. Named for and built near the site of the first Han capital, the new Chang'an emerged as one of the world's great cities under the direction of the Sui Emperor Wen in 582 and then more pronouncedly during the Tang dynasty. During the first half of the eighth century, it could pride itself on a population of about one million within the city walls and another million outside them, and it attracted many merchants and other travelers from distant lands.

Half a millennium later, the Venetian merchant and Silk Road traveler Marco Polo was to dictate an account of a newer capital (Dadu) that highlighted features common to many of China's great cities. Noting a rectangular layout that resembled Chang'an's, he wrote:

> It is twenty-four miles round [and] on every quarter it has a face of six miles. It is all walled with walls of earth which are about ten paces thick below, and more than twenty high. . . . They are all entirely embattled and the embattlements [are] white. There are moreover twelve principal gates, and . . . on each side of the walls there are three principal gates and five palaces. . . . In all these palaces are many very great and wide halls. . . . The whole city is set out by line; for the main streets . . . are so straight and so broad that if anyone mount on the wall at one gate and look straight one sees from the one side to the other the gate of the other side. And everywhere along the sides of each main street are stalls and shops of every kind. And there are about the city many palaces beautiful and great, and many beautiful inns, and many beautiful houses in great abundance. . . . And in the middle of the city there is a very large and high palace in which is a great town clock that has a very great bell, which sounds three times a night.[6]

Such a city far exceeded in size and magnificence anything in the way of an urban settlement one might have encountered at the time in Marco Polo's Europe.

As an expression of the discipline and order the emperor sought to impose throughout his realm, Chang'an itself was constructed in the form of a rectangle, the outer walls of which ran 5.92 miles from east to west and 5.27 miles from north to south. Eighteen feet high and fifteen to thirty feet thick at the base, these walls were pierced by eleven gates, each surmounted by a watchtower. Inside the gates, a visitor from the hinterlands could wander along streets that were systematically laid out in rectangular blocks and lined with houses, shops, and temples. An interior wall surrounded the administrative city. Given over to governmental bureaus, barracks, and other official buildings, this area was the workplace for the academically trained bureaucrats who maintained central authority in areas far from the city. Next to it was the palace city. Here in the Hall of the Supreme Ultimate, the emperor held court.

The palace itself contained the residential quarters of the imperial family and also more administrative buildings and great halls

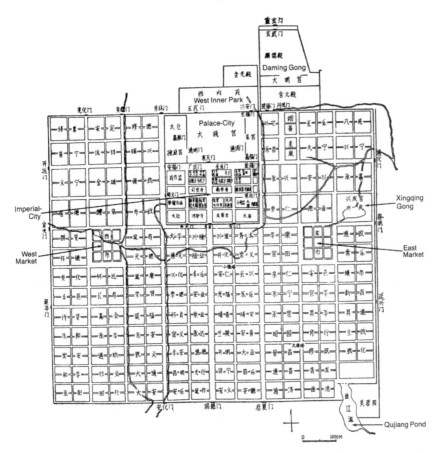

Chang'an was established as a capital city in China in the sixth century ce and reached its height during the Tang dynasty (618–907). The city had a grid-like design that expressed the emperors' desires to project order and stability. The rulers, their families, and their retainers resided in a separate palace city within the larger city. There were also two other palaces: Daming Gong and Xingqing Gong. From Nancy Shatzman Steinhardt, Chinese Imperial City Planning (Honolulu: University of Hawaii Press, 1990), 95.

(one of which measured approximately 425 by 235 feet), all surrounded by a wall 4.75 miles in circumference. Although the city displayed first and foremost the imprint of China's imperial rulers, it also bore impressive witness to the influential presence of organized religion. By 722, the city contained ninety-one Buddhist temples with magnificent halls of worship, bell towers, brightly painted pagodas, libraries full of sacred books, and dormitories and refectories for monks and nuns. Diversity thrived with another sixteen establishments for devotees of Taoism, four for Zoroastrians, and two for Nestorian Christians.

The Tang rulers drew diplomatic delegations from Japan, whose first cities dated from the period 650–700 CE. At approximately the same time, diffusion through commerce with Tang China and India gave rise to cities in what is now Cambodia, most notably the settlement at Angkor, a UNESCO World Heritage site today.

After the fall of the Tang dynasty in 906, Chang'an's population fell steadily, declining to around 300,000 in 1000 and 150,000 in 1500; however, China did not experience urban waning overall. Market towns, county capitals, and imperial capitals were growing. The population of Nanjing (or Southern Capital), which was the capital between 1368 and 1421, likely rose from 180,000 in the twelfth century to 473,000 in 1400. The population of Dadu (present-day Beijing, or Northern Capital), the capital of Mongol rulers from 1271 to 1368 and Ming rulers from 1421 to 1644, rose from 150,000 in 1200 to 672,000 in 1500.

Across the Pacific Ocean, another magnificent capital city laid out according to a carefully designed plan also thrived. Tenochtitlán was established between 1325 and 1345 on an island in the middle of a large but shallow lake as the capital of the Aztec Empire, which was based in central Mexico. Tenochtitlán benefited in particular from commercial routes that brought goods from places as far away as the Gulf of Mexico, the Pacific Ocean, and even the Inca Empire in northern South America, as well as from agricultural goods that were taken from conquered areas as tribute. Consequently, in 1500, Tenochtitlán had a population of at least 80,000 (and some estimate as many as 200,000) inhabitants, making it not only the largest city by far in the Western Hemisphere but also larger than all but a handful of European cities at the time.

Spanish conquistador Bernal Diaz del Castillo described the built-up region in which Tenochtitlán was located with awe:

> When we saw so many cities and villages built in the water and other great towns on dry land we were amazed and said that it was like the enchantments . . . on account of the great towers . . . and buildings rising from the water, and all built of masonry. And some of our soldiers even asked whether the things that we saw were not a dream? . . . I do not know how to describe it, seeing things as we did that had never been heard of or seen before, nor even dreamed about.[7]

Hernan Cortés wrote in a similar vein, with more specific attention to the city of Tenochtitlán itself:

The great city ... is built in the midst of [a] salt lake, and it is two leagues from the heart of the city to any point on the mainland. Four causeways lead to it, all made by hand and some twelve feet wide. The city itself is as large as Seville or Cordoba. ... The principal streets are very broad and straight, the majority of them of beaten earth, but a few and at least half the smaller thoroughfares are waterways along which they pass in their canoes. Moreover, even the principal streets have openings at regular distances so that the water can freely pass from one canal to another, and these openings which are very broad are spanned by great bridges of huge beams, very stoutly put together. ... The city has many open squares in which markets are continuously held and the general business of buying and selling proceeds. ... There are a very large number of mosques or dwelling places for their idols throughout the various districts of this great city ... Among these temples there is one chief one in particular whose size and magnificence no human tongue could describe. ... There are forty towers at the least ... the largest of which has fifty steps leading up to its base: this chief one is indeed higher than the great church of Seville.[8]

In Cortés's, view, the Mexican metropolis compared quite favorably with the largest cities in Spain. It was adorned by "mosques" as well as splendid streets and plentiful markets, all of which testified to a city that was flourishing.

Not long after these words were written, in 1521, Cortes and his men defeated the forces of Emperor Moctezuma II (who had been killed in 1520). After taking control of the city, they largely destroyed it, creating space for a new city of their own. In the meantime, an outbreak of smallpox on the coast of Mexico in 1520 had led by 1521 to an outbreak of the disease in Tenochtitlán, further weakening native resistance to Spanish incursions.

Back home in Spain, Cordoba and several other cities had thrived under Muslim rule starting in the early eighth century, at which time their populations had been much larger than those of cities to their north and east. Cordoba is estimated to have had 160,000 inhabitants around 800 and at least 400,000 by the beginning of the eleventh century.

By the early part of the ninth century, urban centers had once again begun to grow throughout Christian Europe, and the pace of growth quickened after the year 1000. Not counting Spain and Russia, between years 800 and 1000, the number of cities in Europe with populations of 10,000 increased from sixty to 100. During these years, the overall urban population of Italy probably increased by 70 to 80 percent. Partly held back because of ongoing invasions by Norse Vikings, urban

Tenochtitlán was the magnificent capital of an Aztec empire that covered much of Mexico. Built in the middle of a large lake, it was linked to the mainland by several causeways. A splendid square in the middle of the city was ornamented by a royal palace and the Templo Mayor, where human sacrifices were performed. After Spanish conquerors invaded it and destroyed much of it early in the sixteenth century, it became the site for Mexico City. Bpk, Berlin/ Biblioteca Marciana/Alfredo Dagli Orti/Art Resource, NY, ART330306.

growth picked up after the invasions ceased during the tenth century. During the high Middle Ages, between 1000 and 1300, Europe experienced a great boom of city founding and urban development. The number of cities with populations of 10,000 or more grew from 111 to 242, and the numbers of people living in them nearly doubled. In absolute terms, the greatest growth occurred in cities that had long been established. Paris's population, for example, went from 20,000 to 160,000 and Venice's from 45,000 to 110,000.

In the fourteenth century, Europe's population fell by about one-third, as a result of both famines and repeated outbreaks of bubonic and pneumonic plague, starting in 1347. Known as the Black Death, this disease killed huge numbers of city dwellers. In Florence, 50,000 out of a population of 80,000 died during the plague years. In northern Europe, virtually all cities lost between one-quarter and one-half of their populations. Nonetheless, the number of cities with populations of 20,000 or more increased between 1300 and 1500 from ninety-two to ninety-five, and the percentage of the population that was urban (living in settlements of 5,000 or more) continued to increase (from 10.4 to 10.7 percent). In 1500 (if Spain, which at this point was no longer ruled by Muslims is included), there were thirty cities altogether with populations of 35,000 or more inhabitants.

Two areas were particularly marked by significant urban development as a result of their status as producers and/or exporters of cloth and the roles they played in trade and commerce more broadly. These were the so-called Low Countries, which included Flanders, Brabant, and Holland (and such cities as Brussels, Ghent, and Bruges), and northern Italy (Milan, Venice, and Florence). In addition, however, many other places could take pride in urban settlements that were far more numerous, larger, and more developed than their predecessors had been in earlier centuries.

In contrast to Constantinople, Baghdad, Chang'an, and Tenochtitlán, cities in medieval Europe were not founded by hereditary rulers as capitals of large states. They instead arose gradually, as a result of decisions by individuals who chose to live there. These men and women clustered together in fortified areas for protection from rapacious marauders and to pursue livelihoods in trade, commerce, and artisanal production. In general, they also sought to enjoy relative freedom in an ocean of feudal authority and bondage. Indeed, one of the chief features of urban development in medieval Europe was the emancipation of city dwellers from seigneurial control by noble lords (according to the principle that "city air makes one free"), as well as from the power exercised by city-based bishops. This process occurred in tandem with the establishment of communes, local governments in which prominent parts were played by guilds that united urban merchants, more modest tradesmen, and small-scale manufacturers. To be sure, in France and England, townsmen forged alliances with monarchs, who mobilized them in opposition to landed aristocracies in order to heighten the unity and strength of their kingdoms. More widespread, however, were city-states in which populations were largely in charge of their own affairs. City walls symbolized and safeguarded their relative autonomy, especially in the Low Countries and in northern Italy.

One such city was Florence, which became the quintessential site and focal point of the Italian Renaissance and, for a while, the Athens of its time. The humanist scholar and urban official (chancellor) Coluccio Salutati wrote enthusiastically in 1400 about the city in which he lived:

> I cannot believe that . . . anyone . . . can deny that it is the flower, the most beautiful part of Italy—unless he is utterly mad. What city, not merely in Italy, but in all the world, is more securely placed within its circle of walls, more proud in its palazzi, more bedecked with churches, more beautiful in its architecture, more imposing in its gates, richer in piazzas, happier in its wide streets, greater in its people, more glorious in its citizenry, more inexhaustible in wealth, more fertile in fields? What city has been more active in professions, more admirable generally in all things? . . . Where are men more illustrious . . . more distinguished in affairs, valiant in arms, strong in just rule, and renowned?[9]

Posing a series of rhetorical questions to which the answers were supposed to be obvious, Salutati proudly proclaimed his belief that the city he served stood out architecturally and economically. It was also distinguished by the caliber of its leading citizens, who played admirable roles in public affairs.

Founded as a garrison town and administrative center in ancient times, Florence had become a self-governing commune late in the thirteenth century. As such, it was a republican city-state, which ruled over a substantial hinterland that included several other towns. Although elected officials governed Florence, it was dominated politically by an oligarchy of men—often referred to as a patriciate—who also occupied key positions in the city's economy. Florence enjoyed a high degree of prosperity around 1350 that was based largely on the manufacture and sale of woolen goods and on banking. Unsurprisingly, top businessmen also played leading parts in the city's government, often as representatives of the city's rich and powerful guilds.

Although the population of the city dropped sharply in the middle of the fourteenth century as a result of the Black Death, it recovered quickly, and with 61,000 inhabitants in 1400, it was slightly larger than it had been in 1300 (55,000). Moreover, around 1400 and for some time to come thereafter, patrician patronage helped Florence to enjoy a leading position in the cultural life of Italy and also of Europe in general. Pointing to the achievements of its world-class poets, Salutati asked, "Where [else] can you find a Dante, a Petrarch, a Boccaccio?"[10] In addition, the artist Giotto, who painted portraits that were more lifelike than any before, also painted frescoes for some of the city's growing number of churches and chapels and even designed buildings.

During the fifteenth century, although Florence experienced little if any growth in the number of its inhabitants, it thrived to an even greater extent intellectually and culturally. Again benefiting greatly from support that came from men of wealth (particularly leading members of a banking family, the Medicis, whose patronage of thinkers and artists helped to buttress their de facto control of the municipal government), Florence witnessed an extraordinary profusion of creative accomplishment. The most visible sign of this cultural effervescence was a huge cathedral. Designed by the architect Filippo Brunelleschi starting in 1420, this splendid structure included a dome—the largest to be built anywhere since the construction of the Hagia Sophia—that spanned 150 feet and was capped by a cupola that reached 308 feet above the ground. Although his building incorporated many elements of Gothic architecture, other buildings that Brunelleschi designed, such as the Foundlings' Hospital, pointed instead to ancient Roman examples, which became increasingly pervasive as features of Florentine architecture. To this day, painters Leonardo da Vinci and Sandro Botticelli, sculptors Donatello and Michelangelo, and scholars Leonardo Bruni and Marsilio Ficino represent some of the highest achievements in world arts and letters.

After the late fifteenth century, civil strife that resulted from the ascendancy of a religious fanatic named Girolamo di Savonarola, an invasion of Italy by France, and cultural competition that resulted from the growing attractiveness of Rome for artists all worked to bring Florence's great age of artistic and intellectual supremacy to an end. The city was still culturally vibrant (the Florentine composer Jacopo Peri wrote the earliest surviving opera in 1600), but it no longer stood above other cities in the way it had before.

As Renaissance artists flourished in Europe, another flowering took place in West Africa. First settled by an ethnic group known as the Yoruba around the middle of the fourth century BCE, Ife (located in what is now Nigeria) emerged as a city by 1100. During a golden age that lasted for several centuries, it attained a population of 60,000 or more inhabitants. Beautiful bronze, stone, and terra-cotta sculptures were produced there in great abundance, giving evidence of a high level of cultural development. Ife's cultural preeminence lasted until around 1400. Around that time, political and economic power shifted to the nearby kingdom of Benin, which also produced world-class works of art. Bronze and brass statues and wooden and ivory carvings all contributed to the area's aesthetic allure.

Despite the setbacks suffered by many cities in connection with the decline and fall of the Roman Empire in the west, urban centers took root, grew, and thrived between 300 and 1500. Humanity's urban project continued to unfold. The most spectacular developments occurred in the vast area between the Byzantine and the Chinese empires, but cities popped up or expanded in other areas too, such as Japan, Cambodia, and West Africa. In the Americas, by the eighth century, Teotihuacan had grown to at least 125,000 to 200,000 inhabitants from about 20,000 around 350 BCE. Later on, as Tenochtitlán was becoming even larger, small Pueblo settlements such as Anasazi and Hohokam (in today's Mexico, New Mexico, and Arizona) emerged as proto-urban if not fully urban settlements. Living in stone or adobe communal houses that were often built on top of one another in cliffs by the end of the first millennium CE, residents of such places created densely populated villages by the end of the fifteenth century.

CHAPTER 4

Capitals, Culture, Colonization, and Revolution, 1500–1800

In the early modern period, Europe's capital cities expanded rapidly as political centralization redounded to their benefit. As monarchs and nation-states gained power at the expense of competing men and forces, state formation (as well as economic advances) encouraged urban growth. In the area west of Russia and the Balkans between 1500 and 1700, twelve capitals (seven of which were also ports) more than doubled in size, and eight of these more than tripled. Madrid's population rose from 65,000 in 1600 to 168,000 two centuries later; Vienna's rose from no more than 25,000 to 247,000 between 1500 and 1800; and in the same period, Berlin's rose from 10,000 to 172,000. Other European urban centers—among them Naples, Warsaw, Stockholm, Copenhagen, and St. Petersburg—also increased their populations at rates that far surpassed national averages.

In size and influence, Paris and London stood out. Second only to Spain as a nation-state in 1500, France had a capital almost twice as large as that of the next-largest European city (Naples, also a capital). Rising from 225,000 in 1500 to 547,000 by 1800, Paris grew to be about five times larger than its closest French competitor, Lyon. It no longer, however, surpassed London. Whereas Britain had been a relatively minor player on the European scene in 1500, during the following three centuries, it became the leading power on the world stage, and the growth of its chief city clearly reflected its ascendancy. Its population rose from about 50,000 around the start of the period to approximately one million by 1800. London at this point was twice the size of Paris and more than ten times the size of its closest British competitor, the city of Manchester.

London may have grown larger, but Paris surpassed it in beauty. In a book about a journey he made to Paris in 1698, the English physician Martin Lister wrote:

> I did not see the tithe of what deserves to be seen, and well considered . . . however I viewed the city in all its parts, and made the round of it; took several prospects of it at a distance, which when well thought on, I must needs confess it to be one of the most beautiful and magnificent in Europe, and in which a traveler might find novelties for enough for six months for daily entertainment, at least in and about this noble city.[1]

During the seventeenth and early eighteenth centuries, Paris experienced a great building boom. Seeking to overcome the disorderliness that characterized medieval cities, city planners in the early modern period strove for symmetry, order, legibility, and grandeur, following examples set by city builders in ancient Europe and Tang China. Architectural and visual grandiosity served the aesthetic purposes of Louis XIV and also his political purposes. Imposing palaces and other public buildings, long streets that afforded uninterrupted and lengthy views, spacious squares, and other open areas bore witness to the power of absolute rulers and exemplified principles of baroque city planning that had first appeared in sixteenth-century Rome. A new façade was added to the east side of the Louvre palace, the Champs Elysées was laid out, the Champ-de-Mars was created as a parade ground for royal troops, and the Invalides was constructed as a hospital for discharged soldiers. Numerous triumphal arches were also built. Meanwhile, just outside Paris, the most imposing of all palaces was constructed at Versailles, and the rest of the town was redesigned as well.

Frenchmen and foreigners alike admired the architectural enhancements. The English architect Christopher Wren, who spent six months studying in Paris, wrote in a letter in 1665:

> I have busied myself in surveying the most esteem'd fabricks of Paris, and the country round; the Louvre for a while was my daily object, where no less than a thousand hands are constantly employ'd in the works; some laying mighty foundations, some in raising the stories, columns, entablements, etc., with vast stones, by great and useful engines; others in carving, inlaying of marbles, plastering, painting, gilding, etc. Which altogether make a school of architecture, the best probably at this day in Europe.[2]

And what of Wren's own British capital? Originally constructed in 1514 at the behest of Henry VIII, Hampton Court underwent a major expansion, as did Whitehall Palace. Kensington Palace became a royal residence in the 1690s. Following a great fire that destroyed most of London's western part in 1666, Christopher Wren produced a layout that resembled the Paris he so deeply admired. Owners of private property resisted Wren's proposal, forcing most of his plan to be abandoned; nonetheless, a great deal of impressive construction took place according to his designs. A new St. Paul's cathedral was built to replace the old one, and some fifty parish churches were also built in the area around it. Later, also according to Wren's designs, a Royal Naval College that resembled the Invalides in Paris arose as a home for pensioned sailors.

In a book titled *A Tour Through the Whole Island of Great Britain* (1727), Daniel Defoe was just as effusive in his remarks about London as Wren and Lister had been in their earlier comments about Paris. He referred admiringly to "new squares and new streets rising up every day to such a prodigy of buildings, that nothing in the world does, or ever did, equal it, except old Rome in Trajan's time." Defoe gave some attention to palaces and churches, but what most fascinated him were structures associated with economic life:

> The Royal Exchange, the greatest and finest of the kind in the world, is the . . . publick work of the citizens, the beauty of which answers for itself . . . 'tis observable, that tho' this Exchange cost the citizens an immense sum of money . . . yet it was so appropriated to the grand affair of business that the rent or income of it for many years, fully answered the interest of the money laid out in building it. . . .[3]

Defoe here lauded a building whose opulent splendor bore visual witness to the prosperity of the city that was the capital of an economically advanced trading nation.

Paris and London also nourished a wealth of cultural activities not meant just for the elites. Already in the sixteenth and seventeenth centuries, Londoners and Parisians could select from rich arrays of theatrical productions enacted on numerous stages. At the Globe Theater in London plays written by William Shakespeare, Christopher Marlowe, and Ben Jonson were performed starting in the late 1590s. From the 1660s on, Parisians also enjoyed a robust theatrical sector, with plays by Pierre Corneille and Molière. In both cities—except for the years between 1642 and 1660, when English Puritans shut down the London stage—theatrical culture enriched urban life. After the 1670s, public concerts and athletic contests supplemented theatrical offerings.

In the eighteenth century, both cities experienced the growth of public spheres in which writers sought to entertain readers and also enlighten them in ways thought to foster human progress. Paris ranked during this period as the intellectual capital of Europe. Leading thinkers and writers congregated in elegant salons conducted by dozens of upper-class women. Guests enjoyed food and drink, readings, and spirited conversation. Leading writers also met in coffeehouses, which offered magazines and newspapers as bases for informed talk and debate. Stimulated by what they heard, as well as what they read, French intellectuals spread critical ideas that exerted an enormous impact throughout Western society. The most prominent of the philosophes was the indefatigable Voltaire, who spent his youth in Paris and died there an old man after years in exile. Other philosophes—Charles Louis de Montesquieu, Denis Diderot, Jean d'Alembert, and Jean-Jacques Rousseau—spent more time in Paris. These men debated about a wide range of subversive views concerning government, social stratification, and religion.

The Enlightenment also took root in Britain, most notably in Edinburgh, home to the philosopher David Hume and the economist Adam Smith. In London, leading intellectuals did not stand out in the same way as their Parisian counterparts. Nonetheless, the public sphere was vibrant. As author Samuel Johnson said to his friend James Boswell, "Why, Sir, you find no man, at all intellectual, who is willing to leave London. No, Sir, when a man is tired of London, he is tired of life; for there is in London all that life can afford."[4] London's public sphere comprised a coffeehouse culture even more widespread than that of Paris and an impressive number of publications. Publishers produced a dozen London-based newspapers in 1712; *The Spectator*, edited by Joseph Addison, was only one of a growing number of magazines; and London's preeminence in book publishing was indisputable. Between 1710 and 1750, the average number of books published per year in London came close to 1,500 (almost ten times as many as were published in Edinburgh), and in 1750 London accounted for 80 percent of total English book output.

Despite their pleasures, London and Paris were far from perfect. The writer Louis-Sébastien Mercier described the French capital as "a sinkhole into which the whole human species falls."[5] In his *Tableau de Paris*, which appeared in a dozen volumes between 1781 and 1788, he discerned many ills, including the plight of the poor:

> It is almost impossible to be content in Paris, because the ostentatious pleasures of the rich are too visible to the indigent. . . . From the point of view of happiness, the poor Parisian is worse off than a peasant; of all people on the earth, he is the worst cared for. . . . In Paris, one is either plunged into the whirl of pleasure or [into] the torments of despair.[6]

Henry Fielding, an English novelist who was also a judge, was less sympathetic to London's underclass. "Confusion" with regard to one's social position and the possibility of improving it, he wrote,

> reaches the very dregs of the people, who, aspiring still to a degree beyond that which belongs to them, and not being able by the fruits of honest labor to support the state which they affect, disdain the wages to which their industry would entitle them; and abandoning themselves to idleness, the more simple and poor-spirited betake themselves to a state of starving and beggary, while those of more art and courage become thieves, sharpers [swindlers], and robbers. . . .[7]

Much more inclined to blame the poor for the lowly condition in which they found themselves than to express sympathy with them, Fielding depicted a world in which people at the bottom of the social ladder posed a constant threat to good order.

Severe overcrowding and inadequate supplies of clean water contributed to higher urban death rates than birth rates. Nonetheless, because of numerous migrants from villages and the countryside, cities and the urban share of the European population as a whole grew. The number of cities with populations of 20,000 or more (in an area that comprised Russia, as well as the rest of Europe) increased during the period by well over 100 percent, rising from 101 to 221 percent, and the number of cities with populations of 100,000 or more increased from only four to twenty-four. Although these increases resulted in part from population growth overall, cities grew much more rapidly than the countries in which they were located. The proportion of the population of Europe consisting of settlements with 10,000 or more inhabitants nearly doubled, rising from 6.1 percent to 10.6 percent. Overall, European cities grew during the early modern period, although marked fluctuations resulted in severe declines in the size of some cities, particularly during the seventeenth century.

Urbanization proceeded more rapidly in northern and western parts of Europe than elsewhere, particularly around the Mediterranean. The percentage of the population that was urban more than doubled in the north and west, whereas it rose by less than one-third in the Mediterranean area. This difference stemmed largely from the opening up of transatlantic trade routes, which particularly benefited port cities like Lisbon, Bordeaux, Hamburg, Antwerp, Amsterdam, and Bristol. But it also brought wealth and growth to other cities, in a commercial network that stretched across the Atlantic Ocean, from ports to inland areas, and from Britain to Portugal.

The eighteenth-century English artist William Hogarth expressed contemporary fears of lower-class drunkenness and debauchery in an engraving titled Gin Lane. *Many other observers of life in London were similarly critical of what they regarded as unacceptable behavior in what was often referred to as "The Metropolis." Its magnificence was offset in their minds by urban squalor and misconduct.* Tate, Britain.

Already during the early modern period, Europeans greatly enlarged their presence and power overseas. They founded numerous colonial cities, which fostered economic links that contributed to urban growth around the world.

In South Asia, Southeast Asia, and East Asia, cities continued to grow, partly in connection with burgeoning trade and commerce with Europeans but, for the most part, indigenously. With a level of urbanization comparable to or even slightly higher than Europe's around 1300 (while Europe had five cities with populations in excess of 100,000, India had at least six), India had an urban population that increased steadily during the next two centuries. Two cities grew exceptionally fast: Vijayanagara, the capital of a southern Indian empire, rose to half a million in the early sixteenth century, at which time it was one of the two largest cities in the world; Agra, founded as a northern capital in 1506 and future home of the Taj Mahal, grew to over 600,000 by the early seventeenth century. Both of these cities declined sharply in later years. By the end of the period, most of Vijayanagara lay in ruins, while the population of Agra, from which the Mughal rulers had departed, fell to only one-tenth of its earlier size. Other cities, however, arose in their places. Already by 1700, India may have had as many as twenty cities with populations of 100,000 or more, many of which were centers of industry and commerce.

In China too, urbanization had proceeded during the years leading up to 1500 at a steady pace, and cities probably accounted for slightly more of the population there than they did in Europe. Around that time, Beijing (a capital) certainly had a population of more than 600,000, and at least four other cities had populations of more than 300,000. During the eighteenth century, the urban population grew relatively slowly. Nonetheless, in 1800, Beijing was very likely the largest city in the world, its population probably exceeding that of London by several hundred thousand. On a list of the world's twenty-five largest cities, it was joined by six additional Chinese localities, the smallest of which (Ningbo) had 200,000 inhabitants.

Japanese cities, having first emerged between 650 and 700, still accounted in 1500 for only 8 to 10 percent of the overall Japanese population. Already, however, half a millennium earlier, when no European city had yet exceeded 100,000 inhabitants, Nara and Miyako (later renamed Kyoto) had both come close to or exceeded the 200,000 mark, and by 1300, Kamakura had joined their ranks. In the early part of the sixteenth century, scores of additional cities boasted populations of 10,000 or more inhabitants. During the rest of the early modern period, urban growth intensified as powerful warlords (known as daimyos) constructed castle towns, or fortress residences. Over 100 of these became the nuclei of communities that contained merchants, artisans, and samurai (warriors), constituting the foundations of over half of the cities in today's Japan. By 1700, using the 5,000 population threshold as the definition of a city, the share of the population that was urban was 11 to 14 percent, and by 1800, it was 14 to 15 percent. Like India and China, Japan continued to have several very large cities. By the start of the eighteenth century, two of the world's ten largest ones were located there: Edo, later renamed Tokyo, and Osaka. That remained the case in 1800, when Edo, like Beijing, had a population of over a million, and both Osaka and Kyoto had populations of close to 400,000.

Edo began in the twelfth century as a village, where several castles were later built, and began a marked upsurge after the great warlord Tokugawa Ieyasu moved there in 1590 and established a citadel that was intended to protect the city from attack during the later phase of what had been a prolonged period of civil war. Named in 1603 as the Japanese emperor's military deputy, or shogun, Ieyasu and his descendants became Japan's de facto rulers, initiating what came to be known as the Tokugawa period. Consequently, although Kyoto remained the country's official capital until 1868, Edo became Japan's largest city and also the main seat of political power. In the same way that Kyoto had embodied the emperor's earlier claim to occupy the position of political supremacy and in ways that recall baroque city planning in Europe, Edo was now to symbolize the power of the shoguns.

Edo Castle, which was large and magnificent, served as both the structural and emblematic cornerstone of the country's new order. To build it, construction teams in the tens of thousands leveled hills, brought to the city massive granite boulders that were to serve as the castle's walls, and redirected several rivers to form a system of protective moats. With two sets of walls more than fifty feet in height that divided the overall castle into inner and outer sections, with watchtowers that soared above the walls and with a massive inner tower that was visible from miles away, the castle dominated the areas around the city, as well as the city itself.

As the German traveler Engelbert Kaempfer, who visited Japan early in the eighteenth century, put it, "With its many ornamental roofs and decorations the tower gives the castle a grand appearance from afar. So also do the fan-shaped, curved roofs decorated on top and at the end with ornamental dragon heads, with which all buildings are extravagantly covered." Within the walls, there was extensive space for the shogun and his extended family and also for vassals and advisers. As Kaempfer wrote, "Inside the grounds of this castle are the residences of most of the territorial lords. They are arranged along streets and are magnificently built, with heavy gates closing off the outer courtyard. The second, interior castle has ramparts, moats, bridges, and gates superior to the first. . . . In this second castle reside the most senior councilors, the city magistrates, and some of the most powerful territorial lords in beautiful palaces." In addition, the castle's precincts contained attractive areas in which residents and visitors could walk across decorative bridges and through landscaped gardens that testified to the shoguns' good taste, as well as their power and wealth.[8]

The shoguns made numerous infrastructural enhancements. Early during the Tokugawa period, they built wharves in Edo's harbor and several canals. Highways that linked Edo to outlying areas were constructed too. Such infrastructure facilitated construction of urban estates by the shoguns' warrior followers and enabled them to travel back and forth between the city and their rural domains. The biggest driver of Edo's growth was the "alternate attendance" system, according to which the shoguns, in order to ensure the daimyos' loyalty, forced them to spend every other year living in Edo, where they employed large household staffs. In order to tap sources of water more than thirty miles away, engineers diverted rivers and also built a system of canals and underground conduits. The shogunate made further efforts to improve Edo physically following a disastrous fire in 1657 that devastated much of the city. Relocating merchants and artisans from crowded central areas to Edo's outskirts was just one aspect of the shogunate's extensive program for ensuring the safety of the city.

Edo functioned as an administrative center, as the headquarters for Japan's military elite, and also as a central site for the production and enjoyment of culture and entertainment. Samurai strove to keep the traditions of the warrior class alive by riding horses on tracks established for them and by fighting mock battles in which they brandished wooden swords and used blunted arrows. On hunting grounds outside of the city, they caught birds and shot deer and wild boar. But, with a view to becoming effective administrators, samurai also studied Confucian texts (Confucian University having been established at Edo in 1630), wrote poetry, painted landscapes, and patronized the theater.

Merchants and artisans also took part in a variety of cultural pursuits. Publishing houses produced numerous collections of haiku poetry, which was intended to reflect the lives and aspirations of commoners. Dozens of Kabuki theaters also catered to the tastes of commoners, as did the writing of seventeenth-century novelist Ihara Saikaku, who lived in nearby Osaka. The son of a merchant, he authored dozens of

Starting in the seventeenth century, Japanese artists produced numerous woodcuts in which they depicted aspects of urban life. Literary and theatrical culture, as well as artistic culture, thrived. Well-attended Kabuki plays were a form of popular drama that combined singing, dancing, and mime with spectacular staging and costuming. © RMN-Grand Palais/Art Resource, NY, ART466809.

tales about urban life that were widely consumed during the Tokugawa period. In addition, producers of woodblock prints celebrated the milieu inhabited by commoners in works of visual art, establishing a tradition that was to reach its zenith in the mid–nineteenth century in the artist Hiroshige's "One Hundred Famous Views of Edo."

In Southeast Asia, much of which consisted of either islands or seacoasts, a robust network of port cities had existed for centuries. It fostered regional trade and also trade with East Asia and South Asia, Southwest Asia, and the East Coast of Africa. The most important of these cosmopolitan urban centers was Malacca, located in a highly strategic position on the western side of the Straits of Malacca, between Malaya and Sumatra. Cities in the region were not large. Malacca had about 20,000 citizens, but tens of thousands of merchants resided there from time to time as well. Like other port cities in Southeast Asia, it was a city-state with a stronghold that embodied the local regime, as well as mosques and temples, a customs house where commodities were weighed, and a marketplace. Commerce in Southeast Asia's port cities brought together speakers of dozens of different languages, and Muslim migration added religious diversity to the significant presence of Buddhists and Hindus, making these cities among the most cosmopolitan places in the world.

Starting in the late fifteenth century, Portugal had taken the lead in exploring the coasts of Southeast Asia, Africa, and India. In 1510, Portuguese sailors took over Malacca. The Portuguese established a port city in Mozambique, which they had conquered by 1505, and, on the western coast of India in 1510, they took control of Goa. Such ports became the nodal points in a burgeoning commercial system that linked all three continents in the Eastern Hemisphere. The Portuguese were followed by Spaniards (who established Manila in the Philippines in 1567), the Dutch (whose arrival as representatives of the Dutch East Indies Company in what is now known as Indonesia resulted in the founding in 1619 of Batavia, now Jakarta), the French, and the British. In South Asia, representatives of the French East India Company took control of Pondicherry in 1654, and their British counterparts followed suit in Bombay in 1661.

In the central and southern parts of the Western Hemisphere, the European presence became even more pronounced as huge areas came under the direct control of Spain and Portugal, and smaller areas came under French, British, and Dutch control. Mexico City, which was built by Spaniards on the ruins of Tenochtitlán, was one of many cities in Latin America that were constructed after around 1520 in the aftermath of the conquest of the area by men who had embarked for the "new world" from ports on the Iberian peninsula. In Spanish South America, Lima was established in 1535, while in Portuguese-controlled Brazil, Rio de Janeiro was established in 1565. These cities, primarily military and administrative centers, not centers of trade and commerce, were generally laid out according to rectangular patterns that recalled the urban layouts developed in Europe by baroque city planners. Colonial cities in Latin America and European capitals thus became emblematic of the powers of hereditary rulers. Increasingly, however, Latin America also contained mining towns and ports. In Latin America as a whole, the number of cities with populations of 20,000 or more grew from twelve in 1600, to twenty-one in 1700, and to forty-one in 1800, making it one of the most heavily urbanized parts of the world.

Spaniards also established cities in North America (St. Augustine in 1565 and Santa Fe in 1608), but competing Frenchmen and Britons limited their ability to extend their sway. While the French established the cities of Quebec (1608), Montreal (1642), and New Orleans (1718), urban development was particularly noticeable on the Atlantic coast in areas between Canada and Florida. Settlers who came from England and Scotland and their descendants established and nurtured a string of port towns that stretched from Portsmouth to Savannah. New Amsterdam, established by the Dutch as a city in 1653, was taken over in 1664 by the British, who reincorporated it in 1665 as New York. Life in these places revolved around their waterfronts. Wharves and warehouses drew sailors and dockworkers to cheap taverns and well-to-do merchants to coffeehouses. Merchants built substantial homes. Cities and towns were not significant in North America from a numerical standpoint. They accounted for less than 5 percent of the population of British America in 1775. But the urban sector had grown greatly during the preceding century and a half, and by this point, there were twenty or so places with populations of 3,000 or more. Moreover, the largest of these places functioned as centers of commerce and also intellectual life, political power, and political movements.

The foremost city in British North America was Philadelphia. It was established under the direction of William Penn, a Quaker authorized by the British government to serve as the proprietor of a colony that would be known as Pennsylvania. Penn directed officials he appointed to lay out the city according to a careful plan that would provide for regularity, order, and the well-being of the city's inhabitants. He wrote in 1681: "Let the rivers and creeks be sounded in order to settle a great towne. Be sure to make your choice where it is most navigable, high,

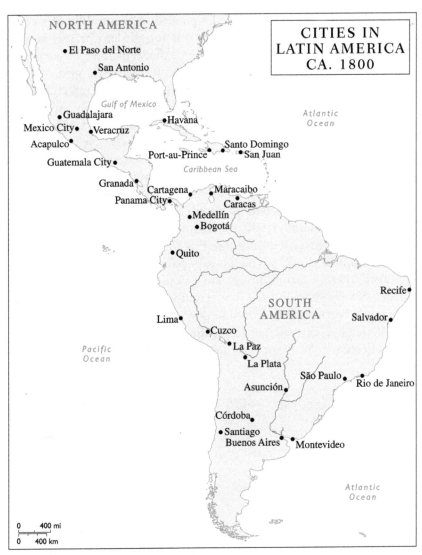

During the early modern period, Spanish and Portuguese conquerors and their descendants established numerous cities in Latin America. The urban network, which extended from Buenos Aires in what is now Argentina to El Paso in what is now Texas, was particularly dense in Mexico and in Central America. Based on a map by Niko Lipsanen.

dry, and healthy. Let every house be pitched in the middle of its plot so that there may be ground on each side for gardens or orchards or fields, that it may be a green country towne that will never be burnt and always be wholesome."[9] Streets were to be formed on a gridiron pattern. The possible monotony of such a design was to be interrupted by five large squares. They served as pleasure grounds and also spaces for civic life, thus contributing to the formation of an urban community. Two major arteries, Market Street and Broad Street, stretched from east to west and from north to south. At their intersection was a market that reflected the importance of trade and commerce in what quickly became a bustling port city, with docks along the Delaware River.

Having occupied second place in the colonial urban hierarchy in 1730, when it had 11,500 inhabitants while Boston had 13,000, Philadelphia far surpassed Boston during the next half century, growing to about 40,000 in 1775. (Boston's population in 1775 was 16,000. New York, then in second place, had a population of 25,000.) Indeed, Philadelphia was at that time the second-largest English-speaking city in the world, surpassed only by London.

Philadelphia thrived economically, demographically, spiritually, and intellectually. William Penn sought to provide a refuge for victims

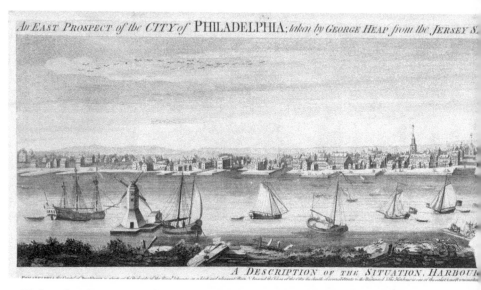

With its bustling port on the Delaware River, depicted here in a 1778 engraving, Philadelphia was at that time the largest city in North America. Containing 40,000 inhabitants, it was a major center of efforts to break free from British rule during the American Revolution and to unify the former colonies as the United States thereafter. Library of Congress, LC-USZC4-12538.

of religious persecution in Europe. According to an English clergyman, in 1759, Philadelphia had places of worship for ten different Christian denominations. Religious freedom and diversity were accompanied by the development of a secular civil society that was marked by both respect for knowledge and robust debate. The American Philosophical Society, founded by Benjamin Franklin in 1743, numbered among its members several outstanding scientists. Knowledge and ideas were disseminated to a wider public in a variety of ways. Many books were imported from Europe, but in the mid–eighteenth century, books were also produced locally by over forty printers (one of whom, until he retired in 1748, was the ubiquitous Franklin). Books became more widely available thanks in part to the rise of lending libraries. In addition, in 1776, the city was served by seven newspapers. Intellectual life was also stimulated by the profusion of clubs, of which there were about fifty in 1750. At such clubs, men sang, pursued hobbies, and discussed and debated public issues. Such exchanges of thoughts and opinions were similarly sponsored by the city's half a dozen volunteer firefighting associations. Taverns, inns, and coffeehouses also brought together men with diverse viewpoints. In all of these ways, an emerging public sphere in the city contributed to growing familiarity

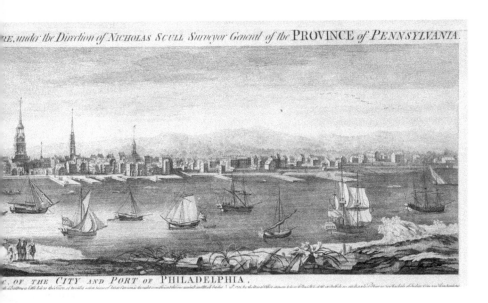

E. under the Direction of NICHOLAS SCULL Surveyor General of the PROVINCE of PENNSYLVANIA.

. OF THE CITY AND PORT OF PHILADELPHIA.

with critical ideas that were being propounded in Europe as parts of the Enlightenment.

Philadelphians helped in other ways as well to pave the path toward American independence and shape the American polity thereafter. Among colonial cities at mid-century, Philadelphia was by no means the most radical. That distinction belonged to Boston. But Philadelphia stood out nonetheless as a major urban incubator of the revolutionary movement. In the early 1770s, its artisans were increasingly insistent on political equality, and their messages were amplified by, among others, the champion of democracy Thomas Paine, who moved to Philadelphia from England in 1774. That same year, the first Continental Congress assembled there. After fighting had broken out outside of Boston early in 1775, a second congress assembled, producing the Declaration of Independence in 1776. Serving as the nation's capital between 1777 and 1788 (except for a brief period of British occupation), Philadelphia hosted in 1787 the convention that produced the American Constitution, and it served as the U.S. capital from 1790 to 1800.

The American Revolution and constitutional government elicited a great deal of admiration from men who sought to bring about political change in Europe, helping to prepare the way for the French Revolution and other instances of urban-based protest. In Paris, where widespread rioting by members of the lower classes had already taken place several times in the eighteenth century before 1789, plebeian discontent became fused with middle- and upper-class protests against both the absolutism and inefficiency of the French monarchy embodied by Louis XVI. When he threatened to disperse a representative body, on July 13, 1789, ordinary Parisians stormed a major symbol of royal power, the ancient prison known as the Bastille. They subsequently murdered six soldiers, the prison's superintendent, and the mayor of the city. Later that year, Parisians forced the return of both the royal family and the National Assembly from Versailles to the French capital where they could be more closely watched and controlled by revolutionaries.

During the next few years, even as members of the National Assembly succeeded in crafting a constitution that greatly reduced monarchical power, repeated outbreaks of popular violence in Paris pushed the Revolution steadily in a more and more radical direction. The storming of the Tuileries Palace on August 4, 1792, resulted in the deaths of over 600 of the king's bodyguards and led to the abolition of the monarchy and the establishment of a republic. Parisians subsequently witnessed the execution of both the king and the queen and a "reign of terror" that was directed against anyone suspected of opposing revolutionary radicalism. As the artisan Jacques-Louis Ménétra put it, "During this time terror hovered over France and particularly in Paris, where everyone lived not only in the greatest penury but also horror of every kind in [the midst of] murders. Everything was in the greatest disorder. The French breathed blood. . . . I witnessed those days of horror and I witnessed all the attacks of the infamous revolutionary committee."[10]

Meanwhile in London, organizations such as the Society for Constitutional Information and the London Corresponding Society spread the democratic word. Men who belonged to these and other groups helped to disseminate ideas contained in Thomas Paine's *Rights of Man* (1791), which celebrated both the American Revolution that he had helped to stimulate and the French Revolution, which he observed. Events in Paris and London thus drew strength from what had taken place across the Atlantic, while at the same time helping to establish a tradition of urban revolutionary protest that would continue to assert itself in both the nineteenth century and the early twentieth century.

CHAPTER 5

Urban Growth and Its Consequences in an Age of Industrialization, 1800–1914

In the early 1840s, a British clergyman named Robert Vaughan wrote, "Our age is pre-eminently the age of great cities. Babylon and Thebes, Carthage and Rome, were great cities, but the world has never been so covered with cities as at the present time, and society generally has never been so leavened with the spirit natural to cities." In a similar vein, writing toward the end of the 1890s, the American statistician Adna Weber asserted that "the most remarkable social phenomenon of the present century" was "the concentration of population in cities." He added that "all the agencies of modern civilization" had "worked together to abolish . . . rural isolation" and to "promote urban growth." Although both of these men recognized that demographic changes had given rise to a multitude of social problems, each celebrated the city as a force that both reflected and contributed to economic, social, and cultural progress.[1]

Particularly in western and central Europe, the United States, and Japan, the nineteenth century witnessed explosive growth in the size of urban populations and in their shares of the total populations of the countries in which they were located. In cities like Manchester, Philadelphia, and Osaka, urbanization was intimately linked to the industrial revolution, but it reflected additional developments too, especially administrative centralization and the establishment of new nation-states. In one such spectacular rise, Berlin increased twelvefold between 1800 and 1910.

Urban growth, which depended to a great extent on an influx of migrants from small towns and the countryside, gave rise to enormous stresses and strains. Overcrowding in small buildings, whose inhabitants all too often lacked clean drinking water, caused terrible public health problems that resulted in high levels of disease and death rates. Declining levels of religious observance and various forms of what was perceived to be deviant behavior by members of the urban masses, together with riots and revolutions, contributed to widespread images of cities as places that were morally as well as physically unhealthy. Increasingly as the century wore on, however, cities served as platforms on which reformers launched programs with a view to rectifying urban shortcomings. To put it another way, cities became social and administrative laboratories, in which increasing numbers of men and women sought to employ goodwill and expertise for the purpose of rendering urban life healthier, happier, and more efficient. As a result of both their efforts and initiatives undertaken by purveyors of popular culture, people enjoyed city life more than ever before.

The overall dimensions of the urbanization process were astounding. In Europe, where the share of the population that lived in cities had remained fairly constant during most of the early modern period, there was a marked change between 1800 and 1910. At the start of this period, only 14.5 percent of the inhabitants west of the Russian Empire lived in settlements that numbered 5,000 or more residents; by the end of it, the percentage had tripled, rising to 43.8 percent. In North America between 1850 and 1910, such settlements increased their share of population from 3.4 to 40.9 percent. What struck contemporaries as being most noteworthy was not the rise of small cities, but rather the rise of what the Germans referred to as *die Großstadt* (the big city). Reaching the threshold population of 100,000 or more inhabitants marked a city as a place that had arrived on the demographic map. Britain led the way. As a result both of the ongoing growth of London and the even more rapid rise of places such as Manchester, Birmingham, and Glasgow, far more Britons than French, Germans, or Americans lived by mid-century in what they called "large towns." But in the century's second half, urbanization picked up speed elsewhere, and by 1910, both Germany and the United States had surpassed Britain in numbers of big cities, with forty-eight and fifty respectively (in the following year, Britain had thirty-nine). At a higher level, there were the cities that had passed the million mark. There were only two such cities in the entire world in 1800: London and Beijing. By 1900, there were sixteen, among which Tokyo—the capital of the rising state of Japan—had displaced Beijing as the largest city outside the Western world.

Gustav Doré's portrayal of people and vehicles crowding a street at the base of London's St. Paul's Cathedral celebrates urban density and vitality. A French illustrator who visited London in the early 1870s, Doré produced dozens of depictions of both high and low life in the British capital. Gustav Doré and Blanchard Jerrold, *London: A Pilgrimage* (London: Grant, 1872). Snark/Art Resource, NY, ART175756.

Just as the Neolithic Revolution had made possible the establishment of the earliest cities, another revolution that involved new techniques of material production sparked the urban upsurge of the nineteenth and early twentieth centuries. The Industrial Revolution began in Britain in the area of textile manufacturing around the middle of the eighteenth century. By the early nineteenth century, Manchester became "the cotton capital of the world." High levels of production in factories were facilitated not only by new sources of power (originally, coal-burning steam engines) and new machines (such as power looms), but also by the division of labor, which depended on large numbers of employees living close to where they worked. The spread of mechanized transportation—above all, steamboats and steam-driven railroad trains—greatly stimulated both industrial and urban development. It enabled manufacturers to produce goods for export to distant markets (which stimulated the growth of port cities like Liverpool, Hamburg, and New York, as well as industrial centers) and also fostered rural-to-urban migration.

Urban growth went hand in hand with the spread of factories in Britain, on the European continent, and in other areas as well. The Ruhr Valley in western Germany was increasingly populated by employees of firms that were involved in heavy industry, producing iron and steel. Such workers added dramatically to the populations of cities such as Duisburg and Essen. In addition to the rapid growth of cities like Pittsburgh, which was also an iron and steel town, Chicago grew astronomically. Among other industrial activities, Chicagoans were engaged in the mechanized slaughter of pigs and the production of pork-based foodstuffs.

Meanwhile, in Japan after the so-called Meiji Restoration that began in 1868, reformers were seeking to modernize their society as a way of defending it against Western encroachment. Their efforts led to an upsurge of both railway construction (by 1887, Tokyo was connected with Osaka) and factory-based production. In 1912, Osaka had 6,145 factories employing over 200,000 workers. According to a 1913 hotel guidebook, these workers manufactured "cotton, wool, oils, ships, matches, machinery, soap, tobacco, medicines, brushes, rolling stock, umbrellas, toilet goods, paint, furniture, paper, candles, canned goods, lacquer, carpets, bags, safes, casks, fans, flowers, musical and sporting goods, ice, clocks, and many other things."[2]

Despite the linkages that are frequently and correctly made between urbanization and the Industrial Revolution, the rise of cities was also (as was the case in early modern Europe) closely intertwined with state

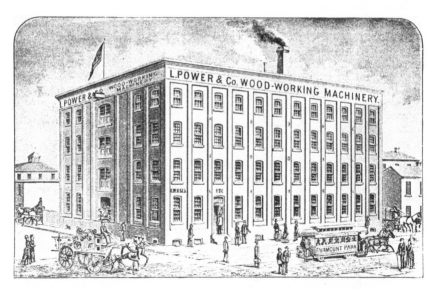

Located in one of Philadelphia's many industrial areas in the late nineteenth century, a factory owned by the L. Power Company produced machine tools that were themselves utilized in the manufacturing process. Horse-drawn vehicles were still widely used, but they were increasingly giving way to means of transportation that were powered by electricity. From Philip Scranton and Walter Licht, *Work Sights: Industrial Philadelphia, 1890–1950* (Philadelphia: Temple University Press, 1986), 51.

formation and other developments at national levels. In the nineteenth century, Europeans witnessed the founding of several new nation-states. Italy and Germany stood out as newcomers on the international stage. But the newly independent states of Greece, Romania, Belgium, and Serbia and a semi-sovereign Hungary within the Habsburg Empire were all places in which certain cities gained greatly in importance because they became national capitals. Rome, Berlin (which grew almost five-fold between 1850 and 1910), Athens, Bucharest, Brussels, Belgrade, and Budapest expanded in part because of their new statuses as focal points for their nations' political life and national administration.

In the United States, where the national government gained greatly in strength as a result of the North's victory over the South in the Civil War, the population of Washington, D.C., tripled between 1870 and 1910, while comparable growth in Tokyo reflected in part the national centralization that was occurring in Japan during those years. Other cities that had been capitals of sovereign states before the nineteenth century also benefited demographically as more and more functions were performed at the national level. Expansion of the roles played by nation-states in meeting the needs of their citizens depended on increases in the numbers of bureaucrats and other state employees, many of whom resided in their nations' political and administrative centers.

Urban growth depended heavily on rural-to-urban migration. Urban birth rates were generally much lower than rural birth rates, and urban birth rates were often lower than urban death rates; therefore, cities (especially big ones) required migrants from the countryside in order to maintain their numbers, let alone increase them. Young men and women who were generally unmarried flocked from rural areas to urban areas. They hoped to find a wide range of opportunities. Heightened possibilities for both personal freedom and economic advancement as a result of relatively high wages beckoned irresistibly to people who (although their families had lived for many generations in the countryside or in small towns) were increasingly dissatisfied with the options available to them. Migrants sought employment in industry, the public sector, or as providers of services for other city dwellers.

Tens of thousands of Irish moved to Liverpool and London, while many Poles made similar treks to cities in the West German Ruhr area. As a result of these and other migrations, around 1850, about half of the residents of all European cities had been born outside the places where they lived. Immigration into cities occurred in the United States on a grand scale, as a result of both migration from the countryside and migration across the Atlantic. Consequently, already in 1890, three-quarters of the inhabitants of New York, Buffalo, Detroit, Milwaukee, Cleveland, and several other large cities had either been born abroad or been born to foreign-born parents.

Particularly during the nineteenth century's first half, the rapid growth of urban populations caused huge problems—some physical or physiological, others moral or political—that, for a long time, local authorities and other leaders could not master. It led to intensified overcrowding, whereby more and more city dwellers lived in what came to be known late in the century as slums. The young Friedrich Engels, who was to achieve great fame as the intellectual and political partner of Karl Marx, described the wretched conditions under which many laborers lived in Manchester (where he was employed in his father's textile business) as follows:

> I may sum up my visits to these districts by stating that 350,000 workers in Manchester and the surrounding districts nearly all live in inferior, damp, dirty cottages; that the streets are generally in a

disgraceful state of filth and disrepair, and that the lay-out of the dwellings reflects the greed of the builder for profits from the way in which ventilation is lacking. In a word, the workers' dwellings of Manchester are dirty, miserable and wholly lacking in comforts. In such houses only inhuman, degraded and unhealthy creatures would feel at home.[3]

Here and elsewhere in his book, a socially observant *bourgeois* assembled material that was to serve as an important part of the underpinning for his and Marx's indictment of industrial and commercial capitalism.

Equally deplorable conditions were evident in other cities in addition to Manchester. In 1861 in Glasgow, two-hirds of the residents lived in one- or two-room flats. These units often accommodated renters, as well as householders and their families, with the result that half a dozen or more people lived in a single, small space. Later in the century, East London became especially notorious because of the large numbers of poor people who were crowded together, their fates having been exhaustively described and analyzed in Charles Booth's massive and classic *Life and Labour of the People of London* (17 volumes, 1889–1903). In 1911 in Budapest, buildings that had been constructed in a working-class area were described as "cells in a prison." In one building, ninety-seven people shared two toilets. Apartments there typically consisted of one room and a windowless kitchen. Overcrowded, substandard housing was also widely apparent in American cities. Reporters like Jacob Riis, who focused on New York City, and novelists like Theodore Dreiser, as well as statisticians and other social scientists, relentlessly documented the problem.

Poorly constructed and overcrowded housing, accompanied by unclean water, streets, and air as a result of the burning of coal, and excessive noise gave rise to horrendous problems in the area of public health. High rates of disease and death followed inexorably as consequences of such conditions. Medical men and other reformers, especially the Englishman Edwin Chadwick, expended much energy in the effort to draw their contemporaries' attention to their cities' unhealthiness. In France in 1848, following several decades of investigation and denunciation by public health reformers there, a socialist by the name of Victor Considérant wrote:

Look at Paris: all these windows, doors, and apertures are mouths which need to breathe—and above it all you can see, when the wind is not blowing, a leaden, heavy, grey-and-blueish atmosphere composed of all the foul exhalations of this great sink. This atmosphere is the crown of the great capital's brow; this is the atmosphere that Paris breathes; beneath it Paris stifles. . . . Paris is a great manufactory of putrefaction, in which poverty, plague and disease labor in concert, and air and sunlight barely enter. Paris is a foul hole where plants wilt and perish and four of seven children die within the year.[4]

In Paris and many other cities, the great killer was cholera, which ravaged numerous cities between the 1830s and the 1860s.

Despite considerable progress between the middle of the century and its end, as urban death rates measurably declined, deep concerns about the physical state of urban populations lingered. In 1890, a British physician by the name of J. P. Williams-Freeman expressed the anxieties of many by asserting that all who could afford to do so ought "to look upon London as we do upon India, or the Straits Settlements, as a rich but unhealthy locality, where, with due care and precautions the well-to-do can remain during the working period of their lives in fair health and comfort . . . but where children can only be brought up with great risk both to health and life." In London, "all attempts to settle permanently from generation to generation only result[ed] in a rapid falling off, both physical and moral, and in early extinction of the race."[5] Many parents in Paris would have agreed. In 1886, the incidence of death among children between the ages of one and five in France as a whole was 30.3 per thousand, but in Paris it was 58.2. In the United States around the same time, the mortality rate for children under five years of age who lived in rural areas was 37.12 per thousand, whereas for children living in big cities, it was 78.0 (89.25 in New York City).

Concerns that had to do with physiological problems were intimately linked, as Williams-Freeman suggested, with moral anxieties. Numerous critics of urban life lamented what they saw as the behavioral consequences of poor health and the prospect of early death. City dwellers, it was thought, sought illicit pleasures in the present in the belief that they would not live to a ripe old age anyway. They also suffered, it was asserted, as a result of a general diminution of social ties and the presence of numerous temptations to seek pleasure at the cost of acting ethically and uprightly. Clergymen were especially intent on identifying and castigating urban immorality. As the American Reverend Amory D. Mayo put it in 1859:

All dangers of the town may be summed up in this: that here, withdrawn from the blessed influences of Nature, and set face to face against humanity, man loses his own nature and becomes a new and artificial creature—an unhuman cog in social machinery that works like a fate, and cheats him of his true culture as a soul. The most

unnatural fashions and habits, the strangest eccentricities of intellect, the wildest and most pernicious theories in social morals, and
the most appalling and incurable barbarism, are the legitimate [i.e.,
inevitable] growth [i.e., outgrowth] of city life.[6]

Clergymen and others had good reason to be worried about the impact
of city growth. One of the primary factors that underlay their anxieties was an overall decline in religious observance that took place
as Europe was urbanized. This decline was much more noticeable in
urban areas than in rural areas. In the view of clergymen, it was quite
natural to characterize the omnipresence of half-empty churches as a
major cause of "moral decay." While not necessarily sharing clergymen's beliefs about declining religiosity, social scientists ratified many
of their concerns. American statistician Adna Weber pointed to sexual
promiscuity, as a consequence of which the percentages of children
born out of wedlock were much higher in cities than in the countryside. He also pointed to relatively high divorce rates. In the late nineteenth century, they were three or four times higher in cities than in
rural areas. In addition, he showed that in 1894, cities in England
suffered from more than twice as much crime, as measured by of-
fenses per 100,000 inhabitants, than did rural areas. Breaking down
such statistics, one can see that although crimes against property were
higher in cities (where there were more goods to steal) than elsewhere,
violent crimes were less frequent. Still, perceptions and fears constituted a force in their own right, and they helped give rise to the belief
that an urban crisis needed to be addressed.

Representatives of the middle and upper classes were apprehen-
sive about putative misconduct by individuals and also riots, strikes,
demonstrations, and revolutions. All of these were seen as being much
more likely to occur in urban settings than elsewhere. Even basically
pro-urban moderates had to admit that urban conditions fostered
popular unrest. In this connection, the French social scientist Émile
Levasseur wrote in 1891 that

[i]n the great agglomerations, passions ferment more. The
working-class masses rise up and furnish flammable material that
tempts the eloquence and the ambition of the tribunes. Political
conditions become less stable. Although there used to be revolutionary troubles in the countryside, there were more of them in the
towns. . . . Today, storms of this kind almost always break out in the
capitals. France . . . has been, since 1789, at the mercy of Paris, which
makes and unmakes governments.[7]

Levasseur presumably had in mind not only the great French Revolution that began in 1789 but also subsequent revolutions that broke out in Paris and Brussels in 1830, in Berlin, Vienna, Budapest, and Milan, as well as Paris in 1848, and again in Paris in 1871 during the period of the Paris Commune. He could not have had in mind but would not have been surprised by the outbreak of a revolution in Russia in 1905 that began in St. Petersburg.

There was other evidence of political discontent in urban areas. In countries to Russia's west, the forces of organized socialism received much more support in large cities than elsewhere. In elections for the Reichstag in Germany in 1898, for example, Social Democrats won 60 percent of the seats located in *Großstädte*, whereas in the rest of the country, they won only 5 percent. Meanwhile, in the United States in 1886, anarchists in favor of an eight-hour workday organized over 1,500 workers in Chicago's Haymarket Square. An attempt by police to disperse the crowd resulted in the explosion of a bomb and eleven deaths, seven of the dead being policemen.

Perceived deficiencies in urban milieus gave rise to a wide range of ameliorative efforts by men and women who sought to mobilize civic energies in pursuit of urban improvement. Much of this activity was voluntary, reflecting the vitality of private associations whose members strove to bring goodwill to bear on urban problems through organized philanthropy. Robert Vaughan wrote enthusiastically in England about such efforts in the 1840s:

> If large towns must be regarded as giving shelter and maturity to some of the worst forms of depravity, it must not be forgotten that to such towns, almost entirely, society is indebted for that higher tone of moral feeling by which vice is in such great measure discountenanced, and for those voluntary combinations of the virtuous in the cause of purity, humanity, and general improvement, which hold so conspicuous a place in our social history.

He asserted that "spontaneous efforts in the cause of public morals, and in the aid of the necessitous . . . are found almost exclusively among citizens." One had to "place in one view with the evils which are generated by the state of society in large towns, the good also which only that condition of society is found competent to call into existence."[8]

Members of voluntary associations of the sort Vaughan had in mind, many of whom were motivated by strongly religious feelings, sought to assist the poor in a variety of ways. They worked, for example, to provide material benefits by raising money and providing care for orphaned children and sick adults. A multitude of umbrella organizations emerged to make charity more efficient and effective. The Charity Organization Society, which originated in London and fostered offshoots in other British and U.S. cities, the Central Office of Philanthropic Works in France, and the German Association for Poor Relief and Charity all arose in the course of the century. Philanthropists attempted to improve the behavior of the poor through educational efforts to elevate them morally, hoping thereby to combat, among other ills, lower-class consumption of alcohol. Privately sponsored education for adults was promoted in particular by men and women who established settlement houses. London's Toynbee Hall (begun in 1884) led the way. In 1889, under the leadership of Jane Addams, Hull-House took root in Chicago. Here and elsewhere, women played a key part in helping to alleviate urban problems through charitable activity.

With ever-growing ambitions during the second half of the nineteenth century and the early part of the twentieth, urban reformers worked to anchor progress in public institutions that operated under the authority of either national or, to a greater extent, municipal governments. Voluntary efforts, they argued, needed to be supplemented by governmental interventions, which would entail both broadened scope and enhanced predictability and permanence. The establishment of professional police forces, as in London in 1829, was one part of reformers' strategies for urban improvement. Two decades later, public health reformers, who had been pushing for improved sanitation since the 1820s, achieved a major victory in Britain in 1848 as a result of the passage of a Public Health Act by Parliament. It gave local authorities the right to take on many new responsibilities. According to the legislation, local boards were empowered to appoint medical officers, pave and clean streets, provide sewers and clean water, and borrow money in order to pay the costs incurred in taking such steps.

A still more sweeping program of urban improvement took effect in Paris during the following two decades under the direction of Baron Haussmann. Appointed to a post as the chief administrator of the French capital by Louis Napoleon Bonaparte (soon to become, like his uncle before him, a French emperor), Haussmann used the powers he was given by his dictatorial patron to make radical changes in the city's layout and infrastructure. Haussmann placed great emphasis on the need to build streets that were straight and broad. Such a layout would enhance the circulation of traffic and prevent insurrectionists from constructing barricades across narrow, winding streets (which had initially stymied the authorities' efforts to maintain order in June of 1848). So that movement on streets and boulevards (one of which, appropriately, was named after him) would not be impeded by railway tracks, he placed the major railway stations outside the city center. Haussmann is best remembered for introducing a feature that was invisible to most of Paris's inhabitants: a vast system of sewers that amounted by 1870 to 348 miles, four times the total in 1851. These sewers did not carry away human excrement. That still had to be removed by hand from cesspits. But by providing for drainage of storm water, these sewers did lead to the improved cleanliness of streets, and along with his other achievements, they greatly burnished his image and that of his city as a center of urban innovation and progress.

In the late nineteenth and early twentieth centuries, dramatic changes in the responsibilities of city governments dwarfed whatever changes had occurred earlier. City-owned waterworks were supplemented by city-owned or at least city-regulated gasworks and electrical works. These works were run as public utilities, though they were not subsidized by payments from the public purse. Profits from their operations—along with profits from governmentally run slaughterhouses and marketplaces—were intended to help finance other urban programs that did not make a profit but were considered to be essential. Mass transit (first in the form of street railways, which were powered by electricity starting in the 1880s and then in the forms of elevated railways and subways) spread throughout municipal areas and also broader metropolitan areas and helped greatly to bind them together. City governments also worked to improve their human capital by constructing hospitals, health clinics, schools, orphanages, and labor exchanges, vastly expanding social services. In some cases, they also built public housing.

In Europe, Britain and Germany stood out as centers of municipal progress. In Birmingham, under the vigorous leadership of Joseph Chamberlain, a far-reaching program of slum clearance, improved sewerage and waste disposal, and construction of public buildings was put into effect in the 1870s. Although Birmingham garnered a great deal of both national and international attention, it gradually ceded its preeminent position to Glasgow, which was described in the 1890s as a "model municipality." Overall, however, it was German cities—such as Berlin, Munich, Frankfurt am Main, and industrial cities in the Ruhr Valley—that enjoyed the most impressive reputations as centers of municipal development. Municipal budgets grew elevenfold between 1870 and 1913, enabling local officials to accomplish a lot. It was with good reason that a German specialist on urban affairs proclaimed in

1903, "We have learned abroad, but foreign countries are no longer our teachers. If one compares what has been achieved in hospital construction, in subway and sewer construction, in park building, and so on in Germany and elsewhere, one can easily assert . . . that we, in these as in so many other areas, have risen to the top."[9]

Advocates of stronger city governments in the United States witnessed the attainment of many of their goals as well. To be sure, numerous observers of the municipal scene—foreigners as well as Americans—were dismayed by high levels of municipal corruption, which manifested itself through graft, the buying and selling of votes, and other forms of official malfeasance (memorably recounted by the journalist Lincoln Steffens in his 1904 book *The Shame of the Cities*). Many reformers continued to feel that their cities lagged behind European cities. But as a result of pushing their countrymen to emulate best practices abroad, they made considerable headway in making their cities better places in which to live. Progressive mayors such as Josiah

The New Town Hall in Munich, the capital of Bavaria, was constructed between 1867 and 1908 in a neo-Gothic style. The style harked back to the Middle Ages, when cities had enjoyed a great deal of independence and power. From Robert Wuttke, ed., *Die deutschen Städte: Geschildert nach den Ergebnissen der ersten deutschen Städte-Ausstellung zu Dresden 1903* (Leipzig: Brandstetter, 1904), II, 28.

Quincy in Boston, Tom L. Johnson and Newton D. Baker in Cleveland, and a host of others helped to bring about major changes for the better in the places where they governed.

Summing matters up, the American sociologist Charles Zueblin pointed approvingly to a record of "municipal progress" that had become particularly pronounced since 1900. What had taken place in the nineteenth century had been good, but what had happened since then had been even more impressive. Zueblin wrote:

> Already this century has witnessed the first municipalized street railways and telephone in American cities; a national epidemic of street paving and cleaning; the quadrupling of electric lighting service and the national appropriation of street lighting; a successful crusade against dirt of all kinds . . . and the diffusion of constructive provisions for health like baths, laundries . . . school nurses and open air schools; fire prevention; the humanizing of the police and the advent of the policewoman; the transforming of some municipal courts into institutions for the prevention of crime and the cure of offenders; the elaboration of the school curriculum to give every child a complete education from the kindergarten to the vocational course in school or university or shop; municipal reference libraries; the completion of park systems in most large cities and the acceptance of the principle that the smallest city without a park and playground is not quite civilized . . . the social center; the democratic art museum; municipal theaters . . . a greater advance than the whole nineteenth century [en]compassed.[10]

In Zueblin's view, cities in America as well as cities elsewhere merited a good deal of recognition on account of the ways in which they fostered a multitude of efforts to cope with urban problems. In the early twentieth century, they were indeed centers of social progress.

Many of the same forces at work in European and American cities were also at work in late-nineteenth- and early-twentieth-century Osaka, the industrial center of Japan. Widespread poverty among urban workers gave rise to a broad range of movements that arose under the influence of Western examples, as Japanese sought to modernize both economically and socially. A municipal corporation that had been created in 1897, when local powers of self-government were granted by the national regime, encouraged philanthropic projects such as support for the poor, medical treatment for Osakans who could not pay for it, and education of orphans. In 1915, the city had 1,585 sanitary associations. Working under municipal direction, volunteer members of these groups sought to combat contagious diseases.

Beyond encouraging socially active voluntarism, Osaka's city government, which was headed by strong mayors, undertook projects of its own. These included extensive renovations of the port between 1898 and 1902, construction of water and sewer systems between 1907 and 1911, taking on responsibility for a modern electric tram and rail system, the introduction of city planning, expanding the municipality's role in the area of education, and investing in health care. Consequently, the number of municipal employees increased twelve times between 1900 and 1920; the amount of money spent by local authorities also rose, from 197,043 yen in 1889 to 9,152,798 in 1908 and to 20,084,725 in 1918. Neither voluntary nor governmental intervention assuaged popular discontent with social conditions, and 1918 was marked by extensive riots. Osaka was, however, turning away from policies that were motivated by the principle of laissez-faire, and after World War I, under the leadership of Mayor Seki Hajime, the city took increased steps toward providing social services, among them the establishment of employment offices, public baths, daycare centers, hospitals, and public housing.

Cities were also centers of cultural activity. In the United States, public official and progressive reformer Frederic C. Howe wrote:

Osaka's port, which was extensively renovated around 1900, accommodated both small boats and larger steamships, linking Osaka to other cities in trade networks. Osaka functioned as a major center of industrial production and commercial exchange as Japan modernized during the late nineteenth and early twentieth centuries. Courtesy of Blair Ruble.

The city has given the world culture, enlightenment, and education along with industry and commercial opportunity. The advance in recent years in this regard has been tremendous. . . . Today, to an ever-increasing mass of the population, opportunities are crowding one upon another. Not only is education generously adapted to the needs of all, but night schools, art exhibitions, popular lectures and concerts, college settlements, the parks, playgrounds, a cheap press, labor organizations, the church, all these are bringing enlightenment at a pace never before dreamed of.[11]

Howe no doubt recognized the importance of governmental support for iconic sites of high culture, such as art museums, theaters, and opera houses, which both contained and architecturally embodied urban elegance. City halls that were constructed in historicist styles (neo-classical, neo-Gothic, and neo-baroque) also stood out as culturally impressive buildings. But what Howe and other champions of cities most admired was taking place in the realm of popular culture.

This culture was fostered in various ways by public authorities, as well as by philanthropic groups. Public schools provided basic education for children. Night schools, often run by private organizations, helped adults acquire new skills and also helped them acquire knowledge that had hitherto been limited to members of the upper and middle classes. Urban governments also sought to promote what leaders and other reformers regarded as healthy recreation. The construction of public parks emanated from a belief among authorities that green spaces in which ordinary city dwellers could amble peacefully with their families on Sundays would promote not only physical but also mental and moral health. One of the major parks in Europe was Victoria Park, established in East London in 1842. In later years, many other cities followed suit. In 1856, for example, New York City acquired the land for Central Park, which was completed two decades later according to the designs of landscape architects Frederick L. Olmsted and Calvert Vaux.

Quite apart from initiatives undertaken by public authorities or with governmental support, most recreational culture was shaped by market forces. Here, consumer culture came to the fore. While only a small minority of city dwellers could afford to go to the opera, many could visit department stores like Bon Marché in Paris, Selfridge's in London, and Macy's in New York, even if all they could do was look at things they wished they could buy. Department stores facilitated the entry of women, who did most of the shopping, into the public sphere. Pubs, restaurants, music halls, cabarets (such as the Motley Theater in

Berlin and the Chat Noir in Paris) also served as vital centers of popular culture. Customers could consume food, drink, music, and dramatic entertainment while enjoying the company of friends. Professional and amateur sporting events also enriched city dwellers' recreational lives. Such opportunities as well as the services provided by public officials contributed to the growing attractiveness of cities in the eyes of the men and women who lived there. Migrants may have been primarily attracted by chances for employment, but they were linked to their new places of residence both economically and emotionally, and their emotional attachments were certainly strengthened by chances to consume and experience popular culture.

CHAPTER 6

Colonial Cities, 1800–1914

In 1908, an anonymous admirer of British imperialism wrote, "World-wide as the colonizing influence of the United Kingdom has been, it is doubtful whether its beneficent results have ever been more strikingly manifest than in British Malaya. The Straits Settlements can look back over a century of phenomenal prosperity under British rule, and the prospect for the future is as bright as the record of the past." Referring in particular to cities, the author continued, "Pinang and Singapore have been the keys which have unlocked the portals of the Golden Peninsula, so that its wealth in well-laden argosies has been distributed to the four corners of the earth." He added that "the spirit of enterprise and progress" had also been diffused in Malaya beyond these cities, as urban and economic development redounded to the benefit of the entire region.[1] Such views were widely contested. A leading nineteenth-century Indian thinker, Swami Vivekananda, accused Europeans of being "intoxicated by the heady wine of newly acquired power, fearsome like wild animals who see no difference between good and evil . . . grabbing other people's land by hook or crook."[2]

Whatever one's opinions about these authors' sharply divergent views of imperialism, there can be no doubt that during the preceding three-quarters of a century, "the colonizing influence" of Britain and also Europe as a whole had been enormous. Following a period of decolonization that began late in the eighteenth century and came to a climax half a century later, Europeans had steadily enlarged their presence outside their native countries. In this process, their control of cities and the fostering of urban growth were crucially significant.

Between the mid-1770s and the early 1820s, a vast change took place in the political status of most regions in the Western Hemisphere in relation to states in Europe. The American Revolution against Great Britain that broke out in 1776, the purchase of the Louisiana Territory from France in 1803, and a series of movements for national independence that emerged around the same time in Latin America under the leadership of Simón Bolivar (known as "The Liberator"), José de San Martin, and others had profound territorial outcomes. They resulted for the most part in the end of European rule between the northern border of the United States and the southern tip of Argentina. Cities throughout the Americas, such as Boston, New York, Philadelphia, Savannah, New Orleans, Mexico City, Lima, Rio de Janeiro, Buenos Aires, and Santiago, emerged from under the shadow of European governance.

In other areas, however, European domination of urban areas persisted and also expanded. Quebec, Montreal, Toronto, and Ottawa remained quasi-colonial cities at least until 1867, when Canada became a self-governing territory in the British Empire. Foreign rule was more pronounced in the Caribbean, where Spain claimed Havana (in Cuba) and Britain claimed Kingston (in Jamaica) and many smaller towns on other islands. Also, in South America, the British established an unofficial empire by means of trade and commerce after the departures of Spain and Portugal.

European power of a direct sort grew greatly in South Asia, East Asia, Southeast Asia, and Africa. Britain gained steadily greater domination over most of India, culminating in a takeover of authority from the East India Company after British troops suppressed a broad rebellion in 1857. In part to justify this takeover, one British soldier wrote to the *Bombay Telegraph* decrying the "hokum" that women and children must be spared. They were "not human beings but fiends, or at best wild beasts deserving only the death of dogs."[3] At the same time, more and more emigrants from Great Britain were populating Australia and New Zealand. France had moved into Algeria in the 1830s and later gained control over Indochina. During the last quarter of the nineteenth century and the first decade and a half of the twentieth, eight European powers carved up almost all of Africa among themselves. European empires came to encompass millions of square miles of land overseas and tens of millions of their native inhabitants. In 1886, a Japanese journalist named Tokutomi Sohō summarized what he described as "an unbearable situation": "The present-day world is one in which the civilized people tyrannically destroy savage peoples. . . . The European countries stand at the very pinnacle of violence and base themselves on the doctrine of force. India, alas, has been destroyed. Burma will be next. The remaining countries will be independent in name only. What is the outlook for Persia? For China? For Korea?"[4]

The relationships between imperialism and urbanization were multifaceted and complex. Members of imperial bureaucracies, such as Lord Curzon, who was the British viceroy in India between 1898 and 1905, and merchants tended to live in cities. Europeans who migrated overseas as nongovernmental or noncommercial settlers were less likely to live in cities, but many gravitated toward what were becoming urban centers. Some colonial cities grew greatly, though most were not nearly as large as European or American cities and grew relatively slowly. In any case, colonial cities functioned as key sites for the projection, establishment, and maintenance of European domination. Most of these settlements were also ports. They played vital roles as intermediaries between the industrializing Western economies and those of the hinterlands, to which they were increasingly linked by roads and railroads. Raw cotton, for example, passed through port cities in India, making its way across the Indian Ocean and through the Suez Canal and the Mediterranean to European ports like Marseilles, Liverpool, and Hamburg. It was transported from there to factories in and around Lille, Manchester, Barmen, and other industrial cities, the growth of which depended heavily on the international exchange of marketable goods. Such raw materials were transformed into finished goods and then shipped back to the cities from which the materials had been exported in the first place. Western domination was not only economic but also administrative and military, and control of cities overseas served as an essential means of maintaining imperial power. In these cities, senior civil servants and merchants had their offices. Armies also had their headquarters in cities. Working together, these forces resulted in a multiplicity of dense networks through which European cities, cities overseas, and their hinterlands were more and more closely linked.

Inasmuch as Britain possessed the world's largest empire, stretching west from New Zealand through Canada, its empire comprised the largest number of colonial cities. Hong Kong, Singapore, Sydney, Melbourne, and Rangoon experienced particularly rapid growth. When the century began, Rangoon, which was the largest of them, had only 30,000 inhabitants, but in 1900, the smallest of them, Hong Kong and Singapore, each had close to 200,000, and both Sydney and Melbourne had close to half a million. Port cities in South Asia also expanded rapidly. Beginning at higher population levels than colonial cities to their east, they widened their leads in subsequent years. In 1900, Calcutta, with a population in excess of one million, and Bombay, with a population of 780,000, led the way, but Madras, with a population of half a million, also deserves mention. In South Africa, although they had to compete for power with descendants (known as Boers) of the

Dutchmen who had settled in the area back in the seventeenth century, the British exercised dominion over both the port city of Cape Town and the inland city of Johannesburg, which grew spectacularly after the discovery of gold there in the 1880s. To the north, although it remained quite small in the nineteenth century, Lagos functioned as a vital port in colonial Nigeria, constituting a foothold that led to its becoming one of the world's megacities by the late twentieth century. Still farther to the north, Cairo became a colonial city when Britain took control of Egypt starting in the 1880s.

The French empire also included colonial cities in Asia and Africa. Starting in the 1830s, large numbers of French citizens migrated to Algiers, nearly doubling its population. Later, also along the coast of the Mediterranean, France acquired Rabat and Tunis. Starting in the century's third quarter, Hanoi and Saigon became linchpins of French rule in Indochina. Even though population growth in these cities over the course of the century remained modest, they served as important bases for the projection and exercise of imperial power.

Other European participants in the race to acquire overseas territories also possessed colonial cities. Batavia, later renamed Jakarta, served as the center of Dutch rule in the sprawling Dutch East Indies (now Indonesia). Spain retained control of Manila in the Philippines throughout most of the century, although this territory (along with Havana in the Caribbean) was lost to the United States in 1898. On the coast of China near Hong Kong, the Portuguese held power in Macao, another port that served as an important nodal point in the network of international trade. Europeans also established lesser colonial towns in Africa, such as Leopoldville (now Kinshasa) in the Belgian Congo.

Along the coast of China, European and American power was extensive enough to be at least quasi-colonial. A series of unequal treaties through which Europeans and Americans forced their entry into Chinese markets linked China's ports to European countries and the United States. In dozens of these "treaty ports," foreigners carved out extraterritorial enclaves, exempting themselves from Chinese law and excluding resident Chinese from participation in city government. Again, the British led the way. After winning the first of the so-called Opium Wars in the mid–nineteenth century, they gained complete control over the undeveloped island of Hong Kong and established their presence in several Chinese cities. The French and Americans joined them in Shanghai, and Germans joined all three to the north in Tianjin. Germany entered Jiaozhou in 1898.

Colonial cities varied widely in their characteristics. To be sure, indigenous urbanization had occurred well before the period of imperialist expansion. On the eve of Britain's arrival in the nineteenth century, the city of Ibadan in West Africa had more than 200,000 inhabitants. Tunis and Cairo in northern Africa and Madras and Hanoi in Asia all boasted centuries of development that long predated the arrival of Europeans. Other cities arose in tandem with colonialism and imperialism. Quebec and Cape Town had been founded by Europeans long before 1800, and Singapore, Melbourne, Adelaide, and Johannesburg sprouted up during the nineteenth century in areas where there were hardly any urban antecedents. Many of the smaller colonial cities in Africa (e.g., Nairobi and Elizabeth Town) were also new creations.

In areas where cities already existed when Westerners arrived, the newcomers had to adapt to local customs, narrow, twisting streets, and high residential densities, as was the case in old Delhi. In contrast, planners could impose their visions of good order on new cities without having to take into account existing settlements. As a result, the planning process in the more important towns led to wide streets that intersected at right angles and standard-sized plots of land. They thus resembled the chessboard patterns that had long been favored by city planners elsewhere starting in ancient times. In addition, space could be set aside for squares and public buildings. Such planning was not universal, but it was more likely in new cities than in old ones.

Cities in settler colonies, where most of the inhabitants were Europeans (or descendants of Europeans), were distinct from cities in which Asians or Africans predominated. Most of the cities in settler colonies, such as Melbourne, were relatively new, although some—such as Quebec and Montreal—dated back to the seventeenth century. Algiers was even older, but after extensive French immigration, only about 20 percent of the population was Muslim. Cities in which the presence of Europeans was relatively small were more likely to be old ones. Even so, because of extensive migration from areas other than Europe, such recently established cities as Singapore and Hong Kong had populations in which the numbers of Westerners were quite small.

The degree to which municipal governments were controlled from without by representatives of foreign powers also varied greatly. The major difference coincided largely with the ratio of Europeans to non-Europeans. No later than the end of the century, city dwellers in places such as Wellington, Sydney, and Toronto—like the populations of the larger territories where they were located—were largely self-governing, the powers exercised there by British authorities being

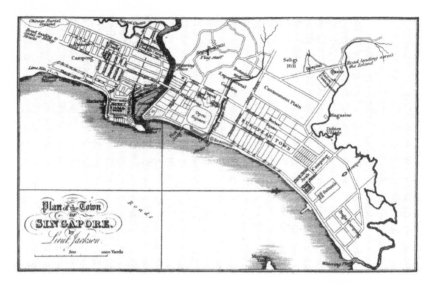

Singapore was established in 1819 by Sir Stamford Raffles, an English employee of the British East India Company. Located at the southern tip of the Malayan Peninsula, the city anchored a growing British presence in Southeast Asia. In contrast to cities whose histories long predated European takeovers, Singapore was laid out according to rectilinear designs. Plan of the Town of Singapore, Lieutenant Philip Jackson. Singapore History Gallery, National Museum of Singapore.

relatively modest. Moreover, municipal institutions were broadly representative of local residents.

Power relationships were quite different in colonial cities that were not located in settler colonies. The mostly nonwhite inhabitants were subject to decidedly undemocratic rule. While political institutions in Europe itself were becoming more and more egalitarian, the hallmark of government in most of the colonies was *in*equality. Convinced of their racial superiority, Europeans took charge of decision-making processes that affected the lives of native peoples, whose numbers far exceeded those of their white rulers. The men who governed these cities reported not to local constituencies but to men who in turn reported to officials in Western capitals. They exercised their administrative authority, among other ways, through the deployment of police forces, members of which were often drawn from areas outside the areas where they worked. Around 1900, for example, 300 Sikhs worked as policemen in Singapore, and many more worked in other towns on the Malay Peninsula. Such men were more willing than native policemen to intimidate members of local populations. Policemen were called on to maintain order on a daily basis but also, in tandem with colonial soldiers, to combat rebellion and civic strife. Having tripled the size of Bombay's mounted and armed police force after a series of riots and strikes, Bombay authorities gave policemen the power to ban a wide range of public activities—among them processions and ceremonies that had led to violent conflicts between Hindus and Muslims.

Imperial administrators were empowered to act in all sorts of ways largely without regard to popularly elected legislators or other natives. To be sure, foreign powers did increasingly establish municipal councils that gradually took on more and more responsibilities. But because members of these councils were often appointed and there were limitations on suffrage that were linked to ownership of property, the composition of such bodies was highly unrepresentative. Saigon, starting in 1877, did have a municipal council, but only two of its fourteen members were Vietnamese. In Rangoon in 1880, Europeans held as many seats on the municipal council as did Burmese, even though Europeans constituted only 3 percent of the population, whereas Burmese comprised 46 percent. In India in the late nineteenth century, only Calcutta (India's capital) had a city council that was elected according to a wide franchise.

Residents of and visitors to colonial cities expressed in many cases the same sense of awe and approval that marked much of the discourse about cities in Europe and America, exuding a belief that these places embodied forces for good. For example, a reporter for the *Australian Home Guardian* wrote in 1856, less than two decades after Melbourne had been established:

> Twenty years ago the site of the Metropolis of Victoria [a colony in which Melbourne was located] was a forest, ten years ago it was covered with a straggling village, today it has assumed the aspect of a city of magnitude and importance; and who shall define the limits of its future dignity and splendor? The prophetic eye beholds its wide and spacious thoroughfares fringed with edifices worthy of the wealth of its citizens and corresponding in architectural pretensions with the greatness of the commercial transactions of their occupants.[5]

What came to be known as "marvelous Melbourne" bore witness to urban dynamism in a far corner of the British Empire, where beauty and wealth went hand in hand.

Later in the century, Lord Harris, the governor of Bombay, expressed enthusiastic delight over

> a great city of 800,000 souls, lying on the shores of a beautiful sea . . . with hundreds of sea-going and coasting merchant vessels

anchored in its harbor, with two busy lines of railways piercing it, with broad thoroughfares and grand buildings, with a most active and intelligent mercantile community both European and native, with its lawns crowded with pleasure and leisure seekers, and its brightness added to by the most brilliantly dressed ladies in the world. . . . Imagine it if you can.[6]

Bombay (now Mumbai) stood out as a densely populated place, in which commerce benefited Europeans and Indians alike and wealth fostered not only architectural grandeur but also leisure and high fashion.

In a similar vein, an Indian intellectual named Rajendralala Mitra waxed eloquently over Bombay's "vitality—its life, energy, and enterprise. Look where one will, whether by day or by night, everywhere he will find men living, and trying to live, and making the most of their earthly career." Giving traditional religion the back of his hand, he added, "There is no Buddha there who plunges headlong into the profoundest abyss of privation and suffering. . . . None is imbued with the pessimism which makes the earth the abode of misery. . . . Everyone is hurrying to and fro, fully alive to the value of time, and everyone is trying to make the most of his capacities and opportunities."[7]

Others writers were less sanguine. In particular, echoing earlier concerns about European sanitation, Europeans and Indians were deeply perturbed by the low levels of public health. Bad enough in normal times (the death rate for Indians in late-nineteenth-century Calcutta as a whole was more than twice that of the Britons who lived there), they took a nosedive during epidemics. In a lecture in Bombay in 1897, a year after the onset of an outbreak of bubonic plague that was to claim almost 184,000 victims between 1896 and 1914, a British surgeon named George Waters bemoaned the illness and death the city was experiencing. "The disease with which we are called on to fight in Bombay," he declared, "is a scourge of the first magnitude, and eminently deserving of the name of plague. It has already done incalculable damage to Bombay, for the blow which this fell disease has done to the great and progressive trade of this port, will, I fear, be felt long after it has disappeared."[8] The British physician William Simpson sought in 1908 to explain unsanitary conditions in Bombay and also in many other colonial cities. Writing in a book titled *The Maintenance of Health in the Tropics*, Dr. Simpson asserted that "[t]he narrow streets, the winding alleys, the crowding together of houses, form an insanitary labyrinth, which cannot be effectively cleansed nor purified by a free circulation of air. The mischief has been done in old towns and frequently to such an extent as to be irremediable without the largest measures of demolition and reconstruction."[9]

Westerners fell victim all too often to diseases that were unknown in Europe and the United States, such as malaria. Colonial officials sought to cope in a variety of ways, primarily to protect the health and welfare of fellow Westerners, but also to combat sickness among natives. Colonial officials advocated and to a certain extent undertook various projects with a view to making their cities more hygienic. In the short run, in order to deal with the plague in Bombay, officials ordered that houses where sick people lived be thoroughly disinfected. Where leaky water pipes led to dampness, water was shut off. Westerners believed that bamboo and other building materials unfamiliar to them harbored diseases, so the authorities tore down such structures.

The only way to improve public health in the long run would have entailed clearing the slums, improving sewerage, and supplying clean drinking water. The creation of the Bombay City Improvement Trust in 1898 led to many enhancements of the urban environment, as did the establishment of a similar trust in Calcutta in 1911. But several barriers stood in the way of implementing such changes, and in general the problems were not overcome. Like measures taken to combat the plague, many other initiatives in the area of public health were regarded as highly intrusive and unwarranted by members of indigenous populations, and they sometimes evoked violent resistance. In addition, European rulers and local taxpayers hesitated to spend the money that proper sanitation required. In New Delhi, constructed after 1912, the government provided ample water and sewerage for public buildings and the homes of government employees. It neglected, however, to take comparable measures in the old, walled Delhi, where most inhabitants of the city lived. In Hong Kong, residents received one-tenth as much water each day as Londoners.

Part of the campaign for upgraded public health included segregating cities by race, sometimes described as an effort to create "dual" cities, with Westerners living in areas from which natives were excluded. Despite the best efforts to raise people of color to an advanced level of cleanliness, so the argument went, they were held back by old habits and perhaps even a congenital inability to do what was needed. Dr. Simpson wrote: "Something more [for urban health than city planning] is required where the races are diverse and their habits and customs differ from one another." The diseases "to which these different races are respectively liable are readily transferable to the European when their dwellings are near each other." It was therefore "absolutely essential that . . . town planning should provide well defined and separate quarters or wards for Europeans, Asiatics, and Africans . . . and that there should be a neutral belt of open unoccupied country at least 300 yards in width between the European residences and those of the Asiatic and African."[10]

Frederick Lugard, a veteran colonial administrator who was devoted to the furtherance of British imperialism in Africa, made the case for segregation even more strongly:

> The first object . . . is to segregate Europeans, so that they shall not be exposed to the attacks of mosquitoes which have become infected with the germs of malaria or yellow fever, by preying on Natives, and especially Native Children, whose blood so often contains these germs. It is also valuable as a safeguard against bush fires . . . which are so common in Native quarters, especially in the dry season in the Northern Provinces. Finally, it removes the inconvenience felt by Europeans, whose rest is disturbed by drumming and other noises dear to the Native.[11]

Wishing to ensure the safety and health of the men and women who were helping to build up the British Empire, Lugard insisted on the need to maintain far-reaching separation between them and the people over whom they sought to impose colonial control.

Segregating Western and indigenous populations was no easier than carrying out enhanced sanitation for entire cities. Both dependence on household services provided by local people and objections by members of local elites, who wished to settle in the best areas they could afford, blurred the lines intended to indicate racial separation in most cities. Nevertheless, numerous attempts to create dual cities met with considerable success. Planners in Singapore divided the city into separate areas for Europeans, Malays, and Chinese. Madras, from an early date, was divided into a "white town" and a "black town." Much later, efforts were made to racially divide cities in Africa—particularly in Cape Town and Johannesburg in South Africa, foreshadowing apartheid. Whites elsewhere in Africa also vigorously pursued racial separation: in Port Elizabeth, Freetown, Nairobi, and Dakar. Meanwhile, particularly but not only in India, the government constructed "hill stations" for Westerners to escape the tropical heat by summering at high altitudes. Simla served as the summer headquarters of the British government for many years. There were many other hill settlements throughout Southeast Asia, such as Dalat in Vietnam. Americans constructed a hill station in the Philippines: Baguio, designed in 1905 by the eminent architect Daniel H. Burnham.

The design and the construction of public buildings reinforced Western rule. Forts, army barracks, police stations, courthouses, prisons, churches, and city halls went up first, followed by lunatic asylums, hospitals, and chambers of commerce. After buildings associated with the maintenance of order came buildings that served cultural purposes: schools, universities, museums, art galleries, and research institutes. Many of these structures were intended to have functional and also psychological impacts. Largely embodying neo-historical European styles (e.g., neoclassical, neo-Gothic, neo-Renaissance), they constituted a pervasively visible form of soft power. The Europeans and Americans who had invested so much time, energy, and money in their architectural projects attempted to constantly remind native city dwellers of their subordinate status and to make it clear that they planned to remain indefinitely.

The French carried out an aggressive and impressive program of building public structures in Indochina. In line with an "assimilationist" view, according to which natives should share in French culture, they exported their architecture vigorously to major cities. In so doing, they ran roughshod over architectural traditions that had deep roots in the area, in both Saigon (the Indochinese capital between 1887 and 1902) and Hanoi (which became the capital in 1902). In Saigon's core, the French constructed an opulent baroque-style city hall that was modeled on the one in Paris, as well as a neo-Romanesque cathedral, materials for which were imported from France, and an elegant opera house. French-style cafes also lined Saigon's boulevards. In Hanoi, in addition to numerous government buildings in various styles and a massive neo-Gothic cathedral, they constructed an opera house that was modeled on the Garnier Opera in Paris and French-style department stores. They named streets and squares after "heroes"—specifically, conquerors of Indochina. Adopted in 1914, a master plan for the development of Casablanca in Morocco led in later years to extensive building in that city as well. In the meantime, the French had made their mark architecturally on many other cities in North Africa.

Britons had a similar impact on major cities in India, but with a somewhat different emphasis. To present themselves as modernizers who were also respectful stewards of native traditions, they sought to blend European traditions with local ones. Accordingly, they built many structures in what was known as the "Indo-Saracenic" style, which drew heavily on Mughal and other architectural styles that had been in use long before the British arrived. In Bombay, the chief building of the university and the massive Victoria Railway Station stood out as examples of this style. Grandiose planning for New Delhi (recently established as the Indian capital next to the old Delhi that

Like Europeans in many other parts of the world, the French who established a dominant presence in Southeast Asia in the second half of the nineteenth century sought to export various facets of European culture. Hoping to spread what they believed was a superior civilization, they constructed many buildings in cities in historic European styles. The French cathedral in Hanoi was built in the neo-Gothic style, which was omnipresent in Europe itself. Courtesy of Chelsea Hicks/Wikimedia Commons/CC-BY-SA-3.0.

had existed for centuries) began in 1911 under the direction of Herbert Baker and Edward Lutyens. Their plan, which took two decades to complete, called for a hexagonally shaped city with wide streets laid out according to geometric designs. The central street, the Kingsway, which was almost twice as wide as the Champs-Elysées in Paris, led up to a huge palace built for the British viceroy, and many other governmental buildings arose nearby. Eventually, a parliament building was constructed downhill from the viceroy's palace, shunted onto a side street. It had not been in the original design. The lack of a democratic meeting place and the rather minimal concessions to Indian architectural traditions (the viceroy's palace was mainly neoclassical) indicate that the construction of New Delhi was intended to both symbolize and uphold British power.

One member of the planning committee who was simultaneously the chairman of the London County Council called for residential decentralization. Referring to ideas expressed by the Englishman Ebenezer Howard in his seminal *Garden Cities of Tomorrow* (1902), he wrote: "I hope that in the new Delhi we shall be able to show how those ideas which Mr. Howard put forward . . . can be brought in to assist this first Capital created in our time. The fact is that no new city or town should be permissible in these days to which the word 'Garden' cannot be rightly applied. The old congestion has, I hope, been doomed forever."[12] True garden cities never materialized. But in residential areas on New Delhi's outskirts, British families were able to live in comfort in bungalows that were built on generous parcels of land.

No such housing was available for most Indians, who inhabited wretched dwellings in cities that had been founded long ago, or for most inhabitants of other colonial cities. In Delhi and elsewhere in colonial areas, both old and newer accommodations for members of the local population left much to be desired. Housing for workers migrating from the countryside was often exceedingly shoddy. In the 1920s, for example, typical housing for manual laborers in Bombay took the form of crude shelters made of palm leaves and flattened kerosene cans that were often shared with domestic animals. More permanent housing resembled military barracks or sardine cans, in which migrant workers were packed and family life was difficult to maintain. Many colonial cities were afflicted by huge gender imbalances. In Singapore in 1871, the ratio of males to females was 3 to 1. In Calcutta in 1911, the ratio was still 2.4 to 1. The colonial city was indeed a man's world.

Imperialism also had a marked impact on the cities in which its forces were headquartered. Imperial cities such as London, Paris, Berlin, Brussels, The Hague, Lisbon, Madrid, and (after 1911) Rome reflected in their public buildings the sense of power and pride that was rampant as a result of imperial conquests. These structures, designed in neoclassical style and sited along broad, straight avenues, were intended to assert similarities between empires of the present and the Roman Empire. Public monuments that celebrated the achievements of supposedly great men who had helped to build the British Empire were especially plentiful in London. In Trafalgar Square, a statue of Lord Nelson, a hero of the Napoleonic Wars, was mounted on top of a Roman-style column, with British lions at his feet, and a statue of Sir Henry Havelock, who had defeated Indian rebels in 1857, was placed nearby.

Immigrants from the colonies came to Europe for various purposes. Some, such as Mohandas Gandhi, sought advanced education, while others sought employment. In the area around the docks in East London, large numbers of men who came from China, India, and Africa worked as stevedores. There was also a large foreign-born population in Hamburg, primarily as a result of the city's international shipping ties, which linked it to areas all over the world. In addition, there were culinary impacts, as men and women who lived in cities learned to appreciate a wide range of new foods, among them curries from India.

Like other areas inhabited by native city dwellers in British India, Bombay was marked by extremely high density, lack of sanitation, and high levels of disease and mortality. Europeans (fearing that they might contract deadly diseases) sought to maintain rigid residential separations between themselves and the natives whom they ruled. From A. R. Burnett-Hurst, Labour and Housing in Bombay *(London: P. S. King, 1925), 30.*

Colonial cities served not only as linchpins in systems of imperial domination, but also as breeding grounds for movements that pointed toward imperialism's overthrow. As in Europe, one feature of the colonial city was an increasingly vigorous civil society. Natives who were educated in schools run by their colonial masters entered into a public sphere. They increasingly viewed themselves as potential citizens who deserved the same opportunities for self-government that more and more Westerners enjoyed. Bombay, for instance, had a university as of 1857 and, by 1900, a dozen other institutions of higher learning, and 451 secondary schools (where English was the language of instruction). By the 1890s, it already had fifty-one Indian newspapers. In this situation, native members of mercantile and professional elites formed a wide range of associations.

Whether they were professional, philanthropic, reformist, or recreational in nature, such associations—in Bombay and elsewhere—helped call into question many of the conventions and customs that had defined pre-colonial societies and also the legitimacy of foreign rule. Colonial cities, as well as cities in Europe and the United States, fostered political movements that pointed toward increased popular participation. In the case of colonial cities, this also entailed movements in favor of national independence. Naturally, the first meetings of the nationalist Indian National Congress took place in India's three major cities: Bombay (in 1885), Calcutta (in 1886), and Madras (in 1887). It was in colonial cities that the foundations were formed for the independence movements that eventually came to fruition on a large scale in the decades that followed World War II.

CHAPTER 7

Destruction and Reconstruction, 1914–1960

> The trains were filled with fresh recruits, banners were flying, music sounded, and in Vienna I found the entire city in a tumult. The first shock at the news of war . . . had suddenly been transformed into enthusiasm. There were parades in the streets, flags, ribbons, and music burst forth everywhere, young recruits were marching triumphantly, their faces lighting up at the cheering—they, the John Does and the Richard Does, who usually go unnoticed and uncelebrated. . . . A city of two million, a country of nearly fifty million, in that hour felt that they were participating in world history, in a moment which would never recur, and that each one was called upon to cast his infinitesimal self into the glowing mass, there to be purified of all selfishness.[1]

So Stefan Zweig, a prominent Austrian literary figure, recalled the excitement at the outbreak of World War I in his autobiography. These young men were swept up in waves of patriotism that life in cities helped to foster. City dwellers, mostly members of the middle class, lined the streets to applaud the young men who were rushing to enlist, ignorant of all the traumatic events to come.

Men, women, and children around the globe who lived in cities during the first half of the twentieth century were to experience a series of profound disruptions. Industrialization, urban growth, political revolutions, and the establishment of European and U.S. control in overseas empires had had far-reaching effects. But events that were to come would be much more violent. Both world wars adversely affected the health and well-being of military personnel and also huge numbers of civilians in urban areas. Cities were much more vulnerable and at risk than small towns and the less densely populated countryside. Wartime hardships also gave rise to revolutionary movements. Both physical damages and revolutions led in turn to ambitious programs of urban renewal.

Urban density and the availability of public spaces made it relatively easy to mobilize people for the purpose of supporting their countries in World War I at the outset of the conflict and also thereafter. Particularly in capital cities, governments and groups of private citizens tried to maintain civilian morale. In London, Paris, and Berlin, huge exhibitions depicted various features of the battlefronts (among them, in the case of Germany, a model trench), with a view to tightening the bonds between civilians and the men who were ostensibly fighting to defend them.

As conflict continued with no end in sight, morale became increasingly problematic among soldiers *and* civilians. Although combat took place almost entirely in nonurban areas, wartime brought considerable hardships to women and children, and also to men who remained at home. These adversities were greatest among civilians who lived in urban areas. During their march through Belgium at the outset of the war, the Germans severely damaged a number of towns, most notably Louvain, where they set fire to the magnificent old library of the university, and to an even greater extent Ypres. Belgrade, the capital of Serbia, suffered severely during and after a successful assault by Austro-Hungarian forces. Consequently, the size of the city's population shrank by at least 90 percent, from about 80,000 to no more than 8,000, and cultural and social, as well as political, institutions ceased to function.

Larger cities suffered from aerial assaults. German light aircraft struck Paris for the first time within a few weeks after the war began. Later, zeppelins, Gotha bombers, and long-distance artillery joined the fray. By the time the war ended, the bombers and the artillery had caused almost 500 deaths and more than 1,000 additional casualties. The worst day was March 29, 1918. A single shell fell on a church next to the Paris City Hall, killing eighty-eight worshippers and wounding sixty-eight. Londoners were also attacked. A bombing of their city in the spring of 1917 resulted in 162 dead and 432 wounded. Altogether during the conflict, at least 1,000 inhabitants of the British capital lost their lives on the home front. British pilots in turn attacked German cities, dropping twice as much explosive tonnage as was dropped on British cities. Measured against the damage done to Louvain and Belgrade and the harm caused by later attacks during World War II, the violence inflicted on Parisians, Londoners, and Berliners during World War I was quite small. It was highly significant nonetheless, forcing city dwellers to recognize that a new age of total war, in which armed conflict was going to affect civilians as well as soldiers, had arrived.

Whereas shelling and bombing directly affected only a few cities on a massive scale and only occasionally, large sectors of urban populations experienced ongoing privations on a daily basis, as the waging of "total" war entailed more and more sacrifices by soldiers and civilians alike. Shortages of food, for example, were endemic in urban areas, occurring most noticeably in the capitals of the major combatant countries in Europe. The problem of such shortages was severest in Berlin and Vienna. In the German capital, the interdiction of shipments from abroad by British ships, the unavailability of the grain that had formerly been imported from Russia, and the drafting of agricultural workers to serve in the armed forces all contributed to acute difficulties, which reached their peak in the winter of 1916–1917. During this period, many Berliners had little or nothing to eat except turnips, the pork and potatoes they had formerly consumed having skyrocketed in price. To be sure, few if any Berliners died of starvation. Nonetheless, malnutrition became increasingly widespread, and it gave rise to sharp upticks in both rates of mortal illnesses like tuberculosis and heightened demoralization, discontent, and general social discord. Similar conditions obtained in Vienna. As in Berlin, the realization that the wealthy continued to eat well exacerbated resentment among the middle and lower classes. A 1918 police report warned: "The public bitterness is directed . . . primarily against the 'rich.' . . . The population harbors deep resentment of the supposed unjust distribution of available [food] supplies."[2]

State and local authorities, seeking to assuage a disgruntled populace and maintain social order, pursued policies that entailed a marked expansion of governmental intervention into the realm of urban society. These constituted an intensification of efforts that had first become noticeable during the latter part of the nineteenth century. Particularly at the municipal level, governmental leaders continued to move away from earlier reliance on the principle of laissez-faire. Assisted by philanthropic organizations, public officials established new practices and institutions that were designed to promote social welfare by providing food, fuel, medical care, and social services to families in need. Much of this assistance was directed at households headed by women whose husbands were in uniform. Rent control and rationing measures also proliferated. All of these forms of social action and many others arose out of the desire to maintain national solidarity.

Such efforts succeeded only to a limited extent. Cities served increasingly as stages for vocal challenges to the war and to the social and political status quo in general. Antiwar demonstrations and strikes became more and more widespread, and some of these actions pointed

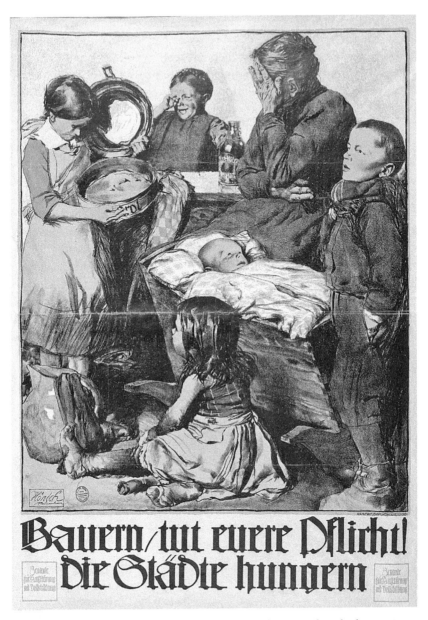

"Farmers do your duty. The cities are starving." These words, which constitute the caption for a poster produced in Germany during World War I, point to the hardships for Central European city dwellers that resulted from the British blockade of German ports. Library of Congress, LC-USZC4-12068.

toward redistribution of political, social, and economic power. Whereas urban milieus had at first fostered pro-war patriotism and continued to do so for a while, what city dwellers, as well as soldiers, had to endure militated increasingly against the maintenance of national unity. As in the periods of urban revolution that had begun in 1789 and 1848, another round of revolutionary action began during World War I.

Revolution occurred in Russia in the first place as a result of the collapse of popular support for the imperial regime, following defeats on the fields of battle and domestic hardships that became particularly onerous and visible in cities. In March 1917, Russian women in Petrograd (formerly St. Petersburg, a city that had long experienced Western influences) protested extensively against shortages of food similar to those in Berlin. Textile and munitions workers went on strike. These protests converged with general war-weariness to erode whatever popular support for the tsarist regime had existed earlier. Unwillingness by policemen and soldiers to forcefully suppress the demonstrators and strikers quickly led to the abdication of Tsar Nicholas II and the establishment of a provisional government, whose members were drawn largely from the ranks of upper-class liberals. The formerly obscure Bolsheviks opposed these men. The Bolshevik leader Vladimir Lenin had returned to the Russian capital in the spring after several years of exile in Switzerland, with a view to using support for the Bolsheviks among members of workers' and soldiers' councils (i.e., Soviets) in Petrograd as a stepping-stone on his path to power. It was there, in November, that the Bolsheviks forcibly displaced the provisional government, whose members were highly vulnerable to Lenin's promises to take Russia out of the war and give both bread and land to the Russian masses.

In *Ten Days That Shook the World*, the radical American journalist John Reed described a mass burial near the Kremlin wall of 500 men who had died in Moscow during fighting that broke out two days after the Bolsheviks seized power in Petrograd:

> Through all the streets to the Red Square the torrents of people poured, thousands upon thousands of them, all with the look of the poor and toiling. A military band came up, playing the *Internationale*, and spontaneously the song caught and spread like wind-ripples on a sea, slow and solemn. . . . A bitter wind swept the square, lifting the banners. Now from the far quarters of the city the workers of the different factories were arriving, with their dead. . . . All day long, the funeral procession passed . . . a river of red banners, bearing words of hope and brotherhood and stupendous prophecies, against a background of fifty thousand people—under the eyes of the world's workers and their descendants forever.[3]

In Moscow, the city served as a stage on which proletarian revolutionaries paid homage to fellow workers who had given their lives in the struggle to establish a new regime.

In several cities to Russia's west, each in a country that—like Russia—had been beaten during the recent war, revolutionary activists sought to emulate the Bolsheviks. After the abdication of the German emperor and the establishment of a republic as the German defeat was becoming clear in the fall of 1918, members of the Communist Party of Germany attempted a coup in January 1919 in the nation's capital. Several months later, Soviet-inspired communists in Munich, the capital city of Bavaria, made a similar attempt to seize power. Meanwhile, in March 1919, the communist Bela Kun seized power in Budapest, the capital of Hungary, with a view to establishing a Soviet-style "dictatorship of the proletariat." Although all of these efforts succumbed to counterrevolutionary forces, they pointed to the potential for revolutionary radicalism in cities after the impact of military defeat.

Although Bolshevik leaders had believed that the survival of their regime depended on successes by fellow revolutionaries outside Russia, they managed, after winning a civil war at home against counterrevolutionaries by the early 1920s, to achieve control over what they renamed the Soviet Union. As a result, they were able to intensify both their assaults against remaining elements of prerevolutionary society and their efforts to build a new one. The promotion of rapid urbanization went hand in hand with rapid industrialization and the movement toward collective agriculture. Hundreds of new cities such as Magnitogorsk, which developed as a major center for the production of steel, sprouted up throughout the Urals and Siberia. Moscow, having become the new capital in 1918, grew from 1.7 million inhabitants in that year to 4.5 million by 1940, largely as a result of industrial expansion.

Moscow's growth was accompanied by bold plans to remake the urban landscape. In November 1935, Lev M. Perchik, who headed Moscow's Planning Department, taunted those who wished to preserve the old Moscow:

> We have completely snuffed out this kind of reactionary opinion and attitude. No one would speak up now in such a way, because millions know from experience that Moscow could not have lived another day in the stone swaddling clothes of its infancy. We still sometimes hear timid voices complaining about the undue severity of surgical methods. Such claims only amuse us. No one has identified a single demolished building which should have been saved; it is easy to find

dozens more which must be demolished. We cannot construct a city like Moscow without a surgeon's scalpel.[4]

A revolutionary regime needed to enact a revolutionary transformation of its capital city. Demolition of old structures would lay the groundwork for urban reconstruction, and such rebuilding would take place.

Although most such aspirations remained dead letters, a prominent example of efforts to improve Moscow's infrastructure can be seen in the construction of the Moscow Metro, the city's underground railway. The first stretch of the Metro, amounting to 11.6 kilometers in length, opened in 1935, and by 1938, further work increased the length of the lines to 26 kilometers. Marked by extensive use of marble (stripped in part from cemeteries) and bronze and richly decorated with statues, stained glass, mosaics, and crystal chandeliers, the Metro stations, as well as the subway cars themselves, made a strong impression on riders, helping to burnish the image of the communist regime as a force for urban progress.

"All Moscow is building the [Moscow] Metro." Construction of the Metro, starting in the mid-1930s, was celebrated in the Soviet Union with pride as a major step toward a more modern society. Contributions made by construction workers and benefits received by ordinary Muscovites received particular attention. HIP/Art Resource, NY, AR931838.

During the years when construction of the Moscow subway was beginning, the threat of aggression posed by Nazi Germany led many observers to conclude that war would once again break out and that—as was already the case in Spain during the Spanish Civil War (1936–1939)—its impact on cities would be quite devastating. In 1938, English author Cicely Hamilton found London in an especially vulnerable situation, "having more noncombatants to be terrorized and panicked" than the capital of any other country with which Britain was likely to engage in military hostilities. In a similar vein in 1939, the medical doctor Sydney Vere Pearson wrote about "the drawbacks of thickly populated areas . . . in times of war or rumours of war when thoughts are turned to air raids and difficulties of food transport." London was "the weakest place on earth . . . the Achilles heel of Britain and of the British empire."[5] While they focused on London, Hamilton and Vere Pearson were pointing to a more general phenomenon: As industrial, political, and cultural centers, big cities became increasingly attractive targets for military planners.

During World War II, the fears expressed by Hamilton, Vere Pearson, and many others were all too fully realized. The impact of hostilities on urban populations was far more direct and far more devastating than it had been between 1914 and 1918. This armed conflict destroyed countless buildings and other urban infrastructures and killed millions of city dwellers, only a minority of them in uniform. The war had a more destructive impact on city dwellers than any war before or after.

Early in the war, the German *Luftwaffe* (air force) took the lead in the *Blitzkrieg* (lightning war), rapidly and extensively devastating enemy urban areas. Warsaw was largely leveled by German bombers within only a few weeks in the late summer and early fall of 1939. As the Nazis shifted their attention in the spring of 1940 to the west, the Dutch port city of Rotterdam suffered similar attacks. As a result of France's quick capitulation and the Germans' decision to vacate the French capital in 1944, Paris was spared such assaults. In contrast, London, Coventry, Manchester, and Liverpool were on the receiving end of German bombs and, later, rockets repeatedly from the summer of 1940 well into 1944. What came to be known there as "the Blitz" leveled huge portions of British towns and killed thousands of people.

Aerial bombardment took a toll that was physical, physiological, and psychological. Although Londoners were determined to "keep calm and carry on," displaying equanimity was often quite difficult, and many of the metropolis's residents suffered from recurring despair.

One woman exclaimed on September 17, 1941, even though her own home had suffered no damage during an air raid that occurred on this particular night, "I can't bear it, I can't *bear* it. If them sirens go again tonight, I shall die." Another Londoner stated, "It's me nerves, they're all used up, there's nothing left of the strength I had at the start." A construction worker described his wife's plight: "It's getting worse than flesh and blood can stand—it just can't be ignored, night after night like this. My wife, I've got to get her out of it, she's getting like a mad woman."[6]

Still greater hardship was suffered by the inhabitants of Leningrad. They experienced a siege that lasted for 872 days, between early September 1941 and late January 1944, when the Germans, finding themselves on the defensive, finally ceased their efforts to annihilate the city's inhabitants. During this period, pain and misery resulted from constant shelling and shortages of food and home-heating fuel. Food scarcity far exceeded what people endured in World War I. A Russian woman wrote in a diary she kept between January 1942 and April 1943: "People are worried and always discussing whether they [government officials] will give us fifteen or twenty grams of herring, ten or twelve grams of sugar. Neither one nor the other will quiet our stomachs. The portions that the blockade will doom us to are less than what is customarily given to a nursing infant as a 'supplement.'" She described the body of a dead man sitting on the snow and leaning on a lamppost near the entrance to a concert hall as "wrapped in rags . . . a skeleton with ripped-out entrails."[7] Altogether during the siege, perhaps a million or more Leningraders out of a prewar population of three million lost their lives as a result of the blockade imposed by the Germans.

British bombers launched strikes against German cities as early as August 25, 1940, and after the United States entered the war late in 1941, the pace of such air attacks picked up markedly. A Berlin-based journalist named Ruth Andreas-Friedrich recorded a night under the impact of enemy bombs in 1944:

> There is a toppling and crashing, quaking, bursting, trembling. To us it seemed as if the floor bounded a yard up in the air. There's a hit. Another. And another. We wish we could crawl into the earth. Biting smoke stings our eyes. Did our neighbors get hit? We have no idea. All that we know is that we are poor, naked, and desperately in need of help. . . . [Finally] All clear! Where the next house stood is now a heap of ruins. A woman runs screaming past us. She is wrapped in a horse blanket; terror distorts her face. Gradually the street comes to life; more and more people appear out of the smoke, the ruins, the

ghastly destruction. They say forty-eight bombs hit our block. The dead can't be counted yet; they're under rubble and stone, crushed, annihilated, beyond the range of help.[8]

Andreas-Friedrich provided a graphic account of what it was like to be a city dweller in a country that (after attacking other countries) was being subjected to aerial assaults by enemy bombers.

Many additional cities in Germany—most notably Hamburg, Cologne, and Dresden—were also heavily hit. Cologne's population of 777,000 before the war declined to about 40,000 in March 1945 due both to loss of life in the city and to flight from the city. After undertaking a continental journey in the summer and autumn of that year, the British author Stephen Spender described Cologne as follows:

My first impression on passing through was of there being not a single house left. There are plenty of walls, but these walls are a thin mask in front of the damp, hollow, stinking emptiness of gutted interiors. Whole streets with nothing but the walls left standing are worse than streets flattened. They are more sinister and oppressive. . . . One passes through street after street of houses whose windows look hollow and blackened—like the open mouth of a charred corpse; behind these windows there is nothing except floors, furniture, bits of rag, books, all dropped to the bottom of the building to form there a sodden mass.

In writing about the people whom he saw on the city's streets, Spender pointed to the sharp contrast behind the recent urban past and the urban present:

These are crowds who a few years ago were shop-gazing in their city, or waiting to go to the cinema or to the opera, or stopping taxis. They are the same people who once were the ordinary inhabitants of a great city . . . when this putrescent corpse-city was the hub of the Rhineland, with a great shopping centre, acres of plate-glass, restaurants, a massive business street containing the head offices of many banks and firms, an excellent opera, theatres, cinemas, [and] lights in the streets at night.[9]

Urban prosperity and elegance had, however, given way to widespread desolation as a result of extensive bombardment of a formerly thriving city, much of which now lay in ruins.

Combat also took a terrible toll on cities in East Asia, where Japan was pursuing a course of violent expansionism two years before the outbreak of war in Europe. In 1937, Japanese forces invaded China, inflicting dreadful harm on Chinese soldiers and civilians alike. Their most notable depredations took place in Nanjing, the Chinese capital.

They executed captured soldiers and tens of thousands of civilians, raping the women before they killed them. The American missionary George Fitch, who was living in Nanjing at the time, described the situation on December 4:

> Complete anarchy has reigned for ten days—it has been hell on earth . . . to have to stand by while even the very poor are having their last possession taken from them . . . while thousands of disarmed soldiers who had sought sanctuary with you together with many hundreds of innocent civilians are taken out before your eyes to be shot or used for bayonet practice and you have to listen to the sounds of the guns that are killing them; while a thousand women kneel before you crying hysterically, begging you to save them from the beasts who are preying on them—and then to watch the city you have come to love . . . deliberately and systematically burned by fire—this is a hell I had never before envisaged.[10]

Such violence and disorder far exceeded anything of this sort that had taken place in any other city heretofore, helping to set the stage for even worse wartime losses of life among civilians in subsequent years. As in Europe, violent aggression by soldiers and airmen was followed by violent retribution, often directed against civilians who had played no direct role in carrying out the acts for which they were being punished. Tokyo suffered a series of air raids, the biggest of which took place on March 9, 1945. On that day, 325 American heavy bombers dropped about half a million tons of explosives on the Japanese capital, with the deliberate aim of causing extensive fires in residential areas. As a result, one hundred thousand residents died, making March 9 one of the deadliest days of the entire war. On August 6, three bombers flew over the city of Hiroshima, dropping an atomic bomb that exploded with the force of 13,000 tons of TNT. Three days later, they detonated a second atomic bomb over Nagasaki.

Over four decades later, a survivor of the attack on Hiroshima named Yamaoka Michiko recalled what she had seen half a mile from the area where the bomb had its greatest impact:

> Nobody there looked like human beings. . . . Everyone was stupefied. Humans had lost the ability to speak. People couldn't scream, "It hurts!" People didn't say, "It's hot!" They just sat catching fire. My clothes were burnt and so was my skin. I had braided my hair, but now it was like a lion's mane. There were people, barely breathing, trying to push their intestines back in. People with their legs wrenched off. Without heads. Or with faces burned and swollen out of shape. The scene I saw was a living hell.[11]

By the end of 1945, the number of those who had perished in the two cities stood at approximately 200,000 (with additional deaths occurring long thereafter as a result of radiation sickness). Moreover, countless buildings had been leveled.

Not all of the big cities involved in the war suffered equally, and some gained. Berliners experienced more destruction than did Londoners, who in turn experienced more devastation than did Parisians. On the other hand, in certain ways, New York City and Detroit benefited. New York grew between 1940 and 1950 from 7.46 million inhabitants to 7.81 million. Like other American cities, New York emerged from the Great Depression due in part to a huge growth in the manufacturing sector, as hundreds of thousands of men and women found employment in war-related industries. The Brooklyn Navy Yard became the busiest shipbuilding facility in the world, with more than 75,000 employees, and it built more battleships than were produced in all of Japan. The city's garment industry, having received a contract for more than 1.2 million overcoats in 1942, continued to produce large numbers of military uniforms. Industrial output also boomed in Detroit, where the population grew from 1.62 million in 1940 to 1.85 million in 1950 (in terms of percentages, a rate of growth nearly three times New York's). Its well-developed automobile industry made it the natural center for the production of tanks and other military vehicles.

The war's aftermath in urban areas where destruction took place imposed clear obligations on men in power. For a long time after the immediate need to provide food, water, fuel, and medical care had been addressed, ways still had to be devised for rebuilding places that remained barely habitable. Public authorities had already begun to devise such strategies during the war; without them, city dwellers could not have returned from the rural areas to which many had fled. Urban reconstruction under the overall direction and with the assistance of the state became a major facet of efforts to repair the damage. In this effort, city planners (often armed with new powers as public servants) played an increasingly significant role.

New housing that could be produced inexpensively was of paramount importance. A leading modernist architect in Germany by the name of Max Taut wrote to Mies van der Rohe in 1948:

> Mostly I think about how one can best and most quickly get a roof over one's head. The smallest and most modest tasks seem to me to be the most important at this moment. . . . We will have to limit ourselves to the most simple building, and even then, before we can

begin [with large-scale reconstruction], which will occur perhaps decades from now, we will have to be satisfied with provisional buildings. . . . I am really not against fantasies and every now and then design "castles in the air," but one must not thereby forget and neglect the true realities.[12]

A prominent example of what such architects found attractive could be seen in a residential quarter known as the Hansaviertel in West Berlin, a showplace of international modernism that was constructed between 1957 and 1961. But the prevailing practice in most parts of urban Europe was to produce houses or apartments that were purely functional and correspondingly cheap, undistinguished, and monotonous. Neither decoratively ornamented nor stylistically innovative, a great deal of such architecture came to characterize both German and other cityscapes in European countries by the end of the 1950s. Other problems also stymied attempts to modernize cities by redesigning them. It was prohibitively expensive to change existing layouts of streets and underground pipes and very difficult to change patterns of landownership. It was simply not feasible to radically transform cities.

Despite high costs, in many cities, building-repair efforts blossomed, most notably in central areas with respect to historic buildings—among them some old residences, as well as churches, city halls, and other public edifices. As early as the 1950s, tourists who visited cities such as Hamburg, Munich, Nuremberg, and Frankfurt am Main, as well as Rothenburg ob der Tauber, were astonished when apprised of the extent to which such places had been damaged during the war. Many buildings looked much as they had looked centuries earlier.

Expenditures for historic restoration were made not only in capitalistic Western Europe but also in Eastern Europe, whose citizens lived under the control of the Soviet Union. In general, communists tended to denigrate advocates of restoration as enemies of progress. Nevertheless, the Soviet government rebuilt the Winter Palace in Leningrad, deeming it a national treasure. Outstanding examples of historic restoration could also be seen elsewhere behind the Iron Curtain. In Dresden, East Germans meticulously restored the Zwinger, a major art museum that had been built in the eighteenth century. At the same time, Poles—armed with public ownership of formerly private land—reconstructed entire blocks of their capital, Warsaw. The city appeared to have emerged from the war almost unscathed, even though 90 percent of its buildings had been destroyed. In the Soviet Union too, major rebuilding took place.

Numerous European cities, including Nuremberg in Germany, suffered severely under the impact of aerial bombardment during World War II. Within two decades after the war had ended in 1945, Nuremberg was largely rebuilt. Much effort went into restoring or re-creating old buildings so that they would appear to have been undamaged. Author's collection.

Muscovites witnessed another sort of divergence from pure practicality. In line with Stalin's efforts to project an image of himself as the heroic leader of a mighty state, the Soviet capital was graced with seven new skyscrapers that were built in a "wedding-cake" style—often referred to as the "Stalinesque" style. Ornate and overblown, these structures reflected Stalin's obsession with grandeur, which was much stronger than any desire to improve the housing of the Russian masses. Such buildings were much less likely to be erected in the democratic and capitalist West than in a state that was ruled by a supreme dictator.

In Japan, urban devastation was as widespread if not more so than in Europe, and here too, the parlous state of the nation's cities cried out for vigorous remediation. In 115 cities that the Japanese government designated as candidates for reconstruction planning soon after the end of the war, burned-out areas comprised nearly 160,000 acres. Over 2.3 million dwellings, formerly inhabited by nearly 9.7 million people, lay in ruins. In Tokyo, most of the built-up area had fallen victim to fire, and some 750,000 houses had been wrecked.

City planners in Japan came up with highly ambitious proposals for urban renovation. A far-reaching plan for radical transformation of the nation's capital issued from the drawing board of the governmental official Ishikawa Hideaki. He called for dividing the city into subcities, each with a population of 200,000 to 300,000, that were to be linked by a network of ring and radial parkways and greenbelts. Because, however, of financial considerations that arose from the need to rebuild outside Tokyo, as well as in it, Hideaki's plan was not implemented; drastic proposals for changing urban layouts also did not come to fruition elsewhere in Japan, the imperatives imposed by existing infrastructures having stood in the way here as in Europe.

In Japan, there was even less modernist innovation and historic restoration than in Europe. So many of Japan's buildings were made of wood that firebombing had left very little that could be rebuilt, and financial constraints were insurmountable in any case.

Even if the results were neither aesthetically impressive nor historically restorative, much effort went into the replacement of structures that had been obliterated by enemy bombers. Although achievements in the area of housing were rather meager during the immediate postwar period, a near doubling of Tokyo's population between 1945 and 1950 followed by an economic boom that began with the outbreak of the Korean War led to marked increases in the construction of buildings. Large apartment houses were erected with governmental support on the city's outskirts. There was also an upsurge in private construction of office buildings in the central city. In subsequent decades, as in European cities, evidence of prosperity became ever more apparent, partly in the form of innovative architecture. Younger generations of Japanese put more and more distance between themselves and their postwar ancestors, although the designation of Hiroshima in 1949 as a Peace Memorial City, with a large Peace Memorial Park in its center, continued as a reminder of what they and their predecessors had had to overcome.

In South Korea, postwar rebuilding was closely linked to the end of Japanese rule and the desire to replace symbols of Japanese domination with expressions of Korean independence. In Seoul, South Koreans tore down one of the largest buildings in Asia, because the Japanese had constructed it, and rebuilt several palaces on the site.

The record of rebuilding war-ravaged areas between 1945 and about 1960 in Europe and East Asia (where extensive rebuilding also took place in Manila, the capital of the Philippines) was truly impressive. Albeit more striking in capitalist democracies than in socialist countries, urban reconstruction added up to a remarkable testimonial to the value that was placed on cities as centers of civilization.

CHAPTER 8

Urban Decline and Urban Growth since 1950

I n *Detroit: An American Autopsy,* the journalist Charlie LeDuff writes about his hometown:

> Today the boomtown is bust. It is an eerie and angry place of deserted factories and homes and forgotten people. Detroit, which once led the nation in home ownership, is now a foreclosure capital. Its downtown is a museum of ghost skyscrapers. Trees and switch-grass and wild animals have come back to reclaim their rightful places. Coyotes are here. The pigeons have left in droves. A city the size of San Francisco and Manhattan could neatly fit into Detroit's vacant lots. . . . Once the nation's richest big city, Detroit is now its poorest. It is the country's illiteracy and dropout capital, where children must leave their books at school and bring toilet paper from home. It is the unemployment capital, where half the adult population does not work at a consistent job. There are firemen with no boots, cops with no cars, teachers with no pencils, city council members with telephones tapped by the FBI, and too many grandmothers with no tears to give.[1]

LeDuff thus uttered a profound lament over the near collapse of what had once been a dynamic, wealthy, and proud place.

In 1950, Detroit's population had stood at 1.85 million, and it ranked as the fifth-largest city in the United States, exceeded in size only by New York City, Los Angeles, Chicago, and Philadelphia. Its citizens could take pride in its prosperity and institutions. Its economic well-being had grown out of its status dating back to the 1920s as the world's leading producer of motor vehicles, the demand for which grew astronomically among American consumers during the postwar years. At the same time, the Detroit Institute of Art stood out as one of the finest art museums in the United States.

Detroit's decline was dramatic. During every decade after its peak, its population fell substantially. According to the census of 2010, since 1950, Detroit's population had declined to 777,000, marking an extreme drop-off of 58 percent, and by 2013, it stood at little more than 700,000. The number of manufacturing jobs in the city had fallen from 296,000 to 27,000. In 2013, 78,000 buildings in the city were vacant; median household income stood at little more than half the median for the state of Michigan as a whole; and 36 percent of the city's inhabitants lived in poverty. The city was further burdened by approximately $18 billion in debt to bondholders, employees, and retirees, a debt the city would clearly never be able to repay. In July 2013, an "emergency manager" appointed by Michigan's governor declared that he was filing for bankruptcy, a request that received judicial approval later that year. The government considered raising money by selling paintings from the Detroit Institute of Art, although doing so would have deeply wounded what was left of the city's pride and done very little to remedy the city's fundamental budgetary problems.

During the second half of the twentieth century and the early part of the twenty-first, other American cities located mainly in the Northeast and the Midwest similarly suffered urban decay. Between 1950 and 2010, the number of residents in Buffalo fell from 580,132 to 261,310; in Cleveland from 914,808 to 396,814; in Pittsburgh from 676,806 to 305,702; and in St. Louis from 856,796 to 319,294. Other cities also declined, albeit not as sharply. Philadelphia dropped from 2,072,605 to 1,526,006 and Baltimore from 949,708 to 620,961. People abandoned their homes, and declining tax revenues made it increasingly difficult for local governments to provide for their cities' needs.

Urban decline resulted in part from deindustrialization, a phenomenon that affected the United States as a whole. The percentage of the workforce engaged in industrial production fell from 35 percent in the late 1960s to 20 percent in the late 2000s. (The same process affected much of Europe too, in Glasgow, the Belgian city of Charleroi, and the German city of Oberhausen.) But the disappearance of industrial employment was most far-reaching in cities that had earlier been industrial leaders, which were increasingly referred to as parts of the "rust belt." Many oil refineries closed in Cleveland, which, like nearby Detroit, suffered from the decline of the automobile industry. Pittsburgh was particularly hard hit by the sharp decline of steel production. The production of locomotives and textiles waned in Philadelphia. Industrial workers in these cities were adversely affected by several trends. Increased productivity resulted in a lower demand for labor. In addition, employers were leaving the Northeast and the Midwest for the South and the Southwest, where right-to-work legislation that was hostile to trade unions enabled them to pay lower wages. Moreover, economic globalization favored products that were manufactured abroad (such as textiles produced for Walmart in Bangladesh), where labor costs were much lower than in the United States. A final factor had to do with taste: the growing preference among many consumers for foreign-made automobiles such as Hondas and Volvos instead of Chevrolets and Fords, which also resulted in jobs being shipped overseas. This trend proved particularly harmful to Detroit.

Deindustrialization was accompanied by intensified suburbanization. Suburbs had originated in the late eighteenth century, when members of the middle and upper classes sought to establish "bourgeois utopias"[2] on the outskirts of London and Paris. Movement by city dwellers just beyond urban boundaries into less densely settled areas picked up steam in the nineteenth century. During these years, street railways and other new means of transportation enabled Americans, as well as Europeans, to commute over increasing distances between where they lived and where they worked.

In the United States in the twentieth century, several developments encouraged moves to the suburbs: growing ownership of automobiles, federally financed construction of highways, federal programs that provided financial incentives for the construction of new single-family dwellings, and a desire among white people to distance themselves from growing numbers of African Americans, millions of whom migrated from the South into Northern cities. Suburbs grew markedly after 1945. Two settlements, each named Levittown (the first constructed on Long Island, the second near Philadelphia), were designed as newly created suburban communities, in which thousands of inexpensive houses all resembled one another. Moreover, many previously established suburbs—Newton outside of Boston, Scarsdale outside of New York City, Riverside outside of Chicago, and Palos Verdes outside of Los Angeles, to name a few—took on added inhabitants. As a result, by 2000, over half of the American population lived in suburban areas, whereas, at mid-century, only a little over one-fifth had done so.

Suburbs were sharply denigrated as well as acclaimed. Jane Jacobs, an influential social critic, subjected them to withering scorn as backwaters of cultural sterility, expressing deep regret over the role their growth was playing in the decline of both unspoiled nature and urban density. She wrote in her classic work *The Death and Life of Great American Cities*:

> We Americans . . . are at one and the same time the world's most voracious and disrespectful destroyers of wild and rural countryside. . . . And so, each day, thousands more acres of our countryside are

eaten up by the bulldozers, covered by pavement dotted by suburban-ites who have killed the thing they thought they came to find. . . . Our irreplaceable heritage of . . . agricultural land is sacrificed for high-ways or supermarket parking lots as ruthlessly and unthinkingly as the trees in the woodlands are uprooted, the streams and rivers polluted and the air itself filled with gasoline exhausts. . . . The semisuburban-ized and suburbanized messes we create in this way become despised by their own inhabitants tomorrow. These thin dispersions lack any reasonable degree of vitality, staying power, or inherent usefulness as settlements. Few of them . . . hold their attraction much longer than a generation; then they begin to decay in the pattern of city gray areas. . . . Thirty years from now, we shall have accumulated new problems of blight and decay over acreages so immense that in comparison the pres-ent problems of the great cities' gray belts will look piddling. . . . Big cities need real countryside close by. And countryside . . . needs big cities, with all their diverse opportunities and productivity so human beings can be in a position to appreciate the rest of the natural world instead of to curse it.[3]

Nonetheless, millions of Americans were continuing to vote with their feet in favor of living in places beyond—albeit not too far beyond—municipal boundaries.

Not all cities suffered. Some older cities did quite well, with both younger people who did not yet have children and older people—all of whom valued urban amenities—moving into central areas. New York City grew modestly and experienced a real renaissance, with marked increases in wealth and declines in levels of crime after what had been a period of great difficulty in the 1970s and 1980s. Despite continuing demographic losses, Boston also flourished, benefiting from the pres-ence of numerous colleges, universities, and world-famous medical in-stitutions. (So too, it must be added, did many cities in Europe, which continued on an upward trajectory after the postwar years of recon-struction. Paris, Stockholm, and Zürich—which came through World War II physically unscathed—and other cities in Europe have enjoyed enviable reputations as attractive places in which to live.)

While some American cities experienced constant decline or at best relatively modest growth, others enjoyed spectacular increases. The cities that grew most rapidly were located in what came to be known as the "sun belt." This area comprises the South and Southwest, its northern boundary stretching pretty much in a straight line from the northern border of North Carolina through the northern border of Arizona and then across southern California. Low wages, low tax rates, the absence of strong labor unions, and, in some cases, the rise of high-technology industries made for a favorable business climate, and a number of cities within this area grew exponentially. Between 1950 and 2010, the population of Charlotte grew from 134,032 to 731,424; of Dallas from 434,462 to 1,197,316; and of San Diego from 334,387 to 1,307,402.

Increases in the percentages of national populations that were urban and in the sizes of particular cities have been largest in areas that were earlier subjected to European and American imperialism. Such areas had long lagged behind their former masters in industrialization and urbanization. They came to be known, however, as parts of the "developing world," a term that generally refers to areas in East Asia other than Japan, South Korea, and Taiwan; in South and Southeast Asia other than Singapore; in the Middle East other than Israel; and in Africa and Latin America. Cities in these places were already becoming more numerous and larger before decolonization. By one estimate, in the developing world as a whole, the number of city dwellers (i.e., inhabitants of settlements numbering 5,000 or more persons) increased from 129 million to 259 million between 1920 and 1950, and these people increased their share of the overall population in the countries in which they were located from 10.8 percent to 15.7 percent. It was, however, during the decades after World War II that the populations of cities outside Europe and North America increased most dramatically. Between 1950 and 1980, urban populations of these areas grew more than threefold, to 905 million, and their share of their countries' total populations almost doubled, rising to 27.6 percent. Percentages of populations that were urban rose most sharply in Africa (10.5 percent to 23.5 percent) and in Asia (from 14.5 percent to 25.2 percent).

During and since the late twentieth century, urbanization has continued in the developing world at a rapid pace. In 1975, 1.5 billion of the world's inhabitants lived in cities, 700 million of them in the "global north" (i.e., the developed world), and 800 million of them in the "global south" (i.e., the developing world). By 2009, the world's urban population had more than doubled (rising to 3.4 billion). Throughout the entire world, the numbers of city dwellers increased markedly. But urban populations increased much more in the developing world than elsewhere, growing in the former area from 800 million to 2.5 billion (212.5 percent), while in the economically more developed world the urban total rose only to 900 million (22.2 percent). Although cities in Europe, North America, and Japan had grown quite rapidly in the nineteenth century, they grew much less quickly in the twentieth century than cities elsewhere. As a result, by 2009, there were many more city dwellers outside than inside the countries that had earlier been most heavily urbanized.

There have been huge changes in both the size of individual cities and the distribution of the largest cities around the globe. In 1950, London was still the biggest city in the world, followed closely by New York. During the next three decades, Shanghai overtook them both. They had fallen respectively to tenth and eleventh places, and—having grown only slightly since 1950 (while the population of Shanghai more than tripled)—they fell by 2013 to the last two places on the list of the world's twenty largest cities. In 1950, nine of the world's twenty largest cities and five of the top ten were located in either Europe or the United States. By 2013, their number among the top twenty had fallen to three, none of which ranked among the top ten.

Similar results emerge from analysis of the world's largest "agglomerations," a term largely synonymous with "metropolitan areas." These agglomerations consist not only of legally defined municipalities but also of the densely inhabited areas around them. Urban historians sometimes cite the numbers of people who live in these larger areas instead of the numbers of inhabitants in areas within cities' official boundaries. The population of greater New York, which had 12.3 million inhabitants in 1950, grew a lot in later years (to 20.1 million), but not as much as the populations of greater Tokyo (36.93 million), greater Delhi (21.94 million), and greater Mexico City (20.14 million). In 1950, Europe and the United States contained eleven of the top twenty agglomerations. In 2010, they contained only two (New York and Los Angeles).

Although a substantial majority of the inhabitants of developing-world countries still lived in rural areas in 2009 (3.1 billion, compared with 2.5 billion city dwellers), the percentages of the populations of these countries that were urban had risen overall by about 100 percent since 1960, and at the level of the giant cities (sometimes referred to as "megalopolises"), the numerical balance had clearly shifted in favor of the developing world. Places like Shanghai, Mumbai, Lagos, and São Paulo have come to the fore as major centers of population, eclipsing in size all but a handful of cities in Europe and the United States.

In approximately equal measure, the growth of big cities in developing countries has resulted from both natural increases (i.e., numbers of births in excess of numbers of deaths) and rural-to-urban migration. Campaigns to reduce tuberculosis, malaria, and other diseases have yielded enormous improvements in public health, substantially offsetting the negative effects of urban density on the ability of

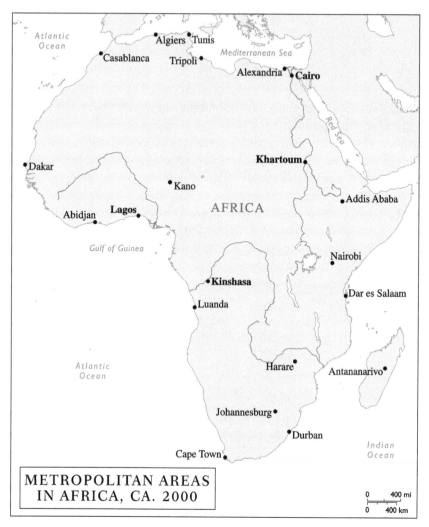

**METROPOLITAN AREAS
IN AFRICA, CA. 2000**

0   400 mi
0   400 km

*Although Europe and the United States took the lead with respect to urban
growth during the Industrial Revolution, cities in other parts of the world
have increasingly come to the fore, particularly since 1945. This map shows
metropolitan agglomerations with two million or more inhabitants. Names in
boldface designate areas that had four million or more inhabitants. Cairo in
Egypt and Lagos in Nigeria—each with a population of over ten million—
were two of the biggest cities in the world.* Based on a map by Niko Lipsanen.

urban populations to reproduce. Increased population density in rural
areas—where birth rates have remained higher than in cities—and
farmers' difficulties in rising above the level of subsistence agriculture
have also played major roles in contributing to urban growth, as a

growing gap between rural and urban wages and incomes intensifies migration. In much of Asia and Africa, decolonization also contributed to urban growth. It did so through the dismantling of earlier restrictions that were intended to limit migration and through the creation of new opportunities for employment in the ranks of civil servants in national and regional capitals.

Additional factors have come into play. Education and mass media have done their parts. In the developing world in 1939, only about one-sixth of all children went to school. By 1960, the total approached 50 percent, and by the start of the 1980s, it stood at more than 85 percent. Schooling helped to extend the horizons and raise the ambitions of young people, who were much more likely than their less well-educated parents to envisage better futures for themselves in places other than the countryside. Mass media, which generally emphasize the positive aspects of city life, had similar effects, as the ratio of television sets to households rose in third-world countries from 1 to 36 in 1965 to 1 to 6 in 1985. Furthermore, new governments in the developing world have actively supported urbanization. Such support has been especially strong in China. After the end in 1976 of the anti-urban "cultural revolution" perpetrated by Mao Zedong and his followers, national leaders took wide-ranging steps to encourage movement into new as well as existing cities. They did so with a view to enhancing their nation's standing on the world stage through economic and social modernization. A final factor has been the skyscraper. Invented in Chicago and New York, the skyscraper now dominates the skyline in such Asian cities as Hong Kong and Kuala Lumpur to an even greater degree than it does in the country where it first emerged. Without it, providing space for all of the people who live and/or work in giant cities would be impossible.

Many observers of urban life have pointed to the downsides and defects of life in the burgeoning cities that have sprouted up in these areas. Observations by writers on the left have been particularly dire. British author and journalist Jeremy Seabrook wrote in the mid-1990s about living conditions in such Southeast Asian and South Asian cities as Jakarta, Saigon, Bangkok, Dacca, and Delhi, expressing a critical view of life in these places that seemed to apply to other parts of the developing world as well:

> Whatever their advantages and consolations, for the most part the slums inflict impaired achievement, ill-health, want and acute discomfort on the majority of their inhabitants. . . . At least 600 million urban residents in the Third World live in life-threatening homes and

neighbourhoods. Many more have no security, [and] run the risk that their homes will be cleared, burned, or demolished by those who have claim to land constantly rising in value. . . . For every story of community achievement, there are as many others of rule by slum lords, drug networks, gangs, and guns.[4]

According to Seabrook, large numbers of people who inhabit the huge cities that abound in the developing world suffer greatly as a result of the insecure conditions under which they live.

In 2006, Mike Davis, an influential social critic, as well as a theorist, indicted a "planet of slums." After drawing examples from Bangkok, Beijing, Dacca, Delhi, Istanbul, Jakarta, Karachi, and Shanghai in Asia; Cairo, Nairobi, Lagos, Luanda, and Kinshasa in Africa; and Mexico City, Bogotà, Caracas, São Paulo, Rio de Janeiro, and Buenos Aires in Latin America, Davis summarizes his critique by writing:

> The cities of the future [i.e., the ones in the developing world on which he concentrates] rather than being made out of glass and steel as envisaged by earlier generations of urbanists, are instead constructed out of crude brick, straw, recycled plastic, cement blocks, and scrap wood. Instead of cities of light soaring toward heaven, much of the twenty-first-century urban world squats in squalor, surrounded by pollution, excrement, and decay. Indeed, the one billion city-dwellers who inhabit postmodern slums might well look back with envy at the ruins of the sturdy mud homes of Çatal Hüyük in Anatolia, erected at the very dawn of city life nine thousand years ago.[5]

Davis's view is even more dire than Seabrook's. Painting a highly negative picture of urban conditions, he relentlessly emphasizes dirt, disease, and decay in large parts of the cities in developing areas.

The extent and effects of overcrowded and dilapidated housing and homelessness on hundreds of millions of slum dwellers who live in poverty and in filth have been particularly severe. These people, whose numbers grew faster than the numbers of city dwellers overall (constituting over 30 percent of the world's urban population by 2000), contend with a multitude of extreme hardships. Already in 1967, a group of foreign urbanists who had been invited to visit Calcutta declared, "We have not seen human degradation on a comparable scale in any other city in the world. This is a matter of one of the greatest urban concentrations in existence rapidly approaching the point of breakdown in terms of its economy, housing, sanitation, transport, and the essential humanities of life. If the final breakdown were to take place it would be a disaster for mankind of a more sinister sort than any disaster of flood or famine."[6]

Nearly four decades later, a horrified British journalist reported about slumlike conditions in one of the largest cities in Africa: "In a squeezed square mile on the south-western outskirts of Nairobi, Kibera is home to nearly one million people—a third of the city's population. Most of them live in one-room mud or wattle huts or in wooden or basic stone houses, often windowless. . . . The Kenyan state provides the huge, illegal sprawl with nothing—no sanitation, no roads, no hospitals. It is a massive ditch of mud and filth, with a brown dribble of a stream running through it."[7]

In Latin American cities, where the share of the urban population that was considered to be poor amounted to one-third in 2009, overcrowding has been quite widespread. In São Paulo and Rio de Janeiro, slum residences that are known as *favelas* (shantytowns) have been built on steep hillsides outside city centers. Although their impoverished inhabitants live on the urban peripheries, they are close enough to the imposing structures that mark the centers of these cities to be able to compare their lot with that of their more prosperous fellow citizens.

This Rio de Janeiro favela (slum in Portuguese) stands out as an area of high-density living in which there are few city services. Favelas *often abut much more prosperous areas.* Album/Art Resource, NY, alb1466790.

As was the case in European and American slums in the nineteenth century, life in a third-world slum in the twenty-first century—and life in megacities in the developing world in general—entails constant exposure to daunting threats to the inhabitants' bodily health. Residents of *favelas*, where buildings lack proper foundations, run the risk of seeing their hastily built shacks washed downhill during rainstorms. But the main problem for slum-dwellers is an insufficiency of clean water. As Davis points out, "A staggering 40 percent of total mortality [in Mumbai] is attributed to infections and parasitic diseases arising from water contamination and wretched sanitation."[8] In combination with deficient sewerage, the lack of safe drinking water kills many city dwellers. In Nairobi, for example, the death rate among children under the age of five who live in the city's slums is two to three times higher than that of the city as a whole. In Mumbai, where there are no toilets in some slums, and there is only one toilet for ninety-four people in others, death rates were 50 percent higher than in adjoining rural districts around 2000.

The decreased quality of the air that city dwellers breathe in the new giant cities is increasingly worrisome. Rampant motorization has had and is having deleterious effects in many cities. Seeking to catch up with the relatively high levels of consumption enjoyed by inhabitants of the developed world, city dwellers elsewhere purchase large numbers of automobiles. Many of these are relatively older, inexpensive vehicles that burn gasoline much less efficiently than more modern cars. There are other sources of filthy air as well. In Mexico City in the late 1990s, millions of residents suffered from air pollution that resulted from emissions caused by three million motor vehicles and a host of additional factors. In areas that suffered from deforestation and erosion as a result of new construction on hillsides, high winds whipped up loose earth and turned it into airborne dust. Emissions from factories and odors from human excrement and other waste also had deleterious effects. At one point in the early 1990s, air quality was so poor that Mexico City's mayor declared a four-week state of environmental emergency.

More recently, the growing presence of automobiles and other factors that produce excessive smog has had particularly harmful effects on Chinese cities. *New York Times* columnist Thomas L. Friedman reported in November 2013 about "a perfect storm of pollution in the northeastern industrial city of Harbin, home to 10 million people. It was so bad that bus drivers were getting lost because the smog-enveloped roads would only permit them to see a few yards ahead. Harbin's official website reportedly warned that 'cars with headlights turned on were moving no faster than pedestrians and honking frequently as drivers struggled to see traffic lights meters away.' "[9] The case of Harbin is an extreme example of a phenomenon that is constantly, if less dramatically, present elsewhere. It is often difficult to see for more than half a mile in Beijing and Shanghai.

Still, densely settled urban areas can be centers and motivators of economic, social, and cultural progress. Economist Edward Glaeser celebrates "the triumph of the city":

> I suspect that in the long run, the twentieth-century fling with suburban living will look, just like the brief age of the industrial city, more like an aberration than a trend. Building cities is difficult and density creates costs as well as benefits. But those costs are well worth bearing, because whether in London's ornate arcades or Rio's fractious favelas, whether in the high-rises of Hong Kong or the dusty workspaces of Dharavi [a slum area in Mumbai], our culture, our prosperity, and our freedom are all ultimately gifts of people living, working, and thinking together—the ultimate triumph of the city.[10]

With more and more Chinese crowding into newly constructed apartment buildings, cities in China (such as Beijing, shown here) are beset by both swelling traffic congestion and polluted air. As cars replace bicycles and coal is used more and more, rapidly growing numbers of city dwellers find it harder and harder to breathe. Photo by Robert Lyons.

Innovations fostered by city dwellers, Glaeser argues, benefit society as a whole.[11] Overall urban growth has led to greater wealth in the form of higher income per capita and also to higher levels of happiness. Glaeser even asks rhetorically, "What's good about slums?" He answers this question in part by arguing that, instead of being poor because they live in slums, poor people move to and stay in these areas because they rightly believe that their chances of escaping poverty are much better there than in nonurban areas. He writes, "Urban poverty is not pretty—no poverty is pretty—but the favelas of Rio, the slums of Mumbai, and the ghettos of Chicago have long provided pathways out of destitution for the poor."[12]

Civic boosters today echo their nineteenth-century European and American predecessors. They also echo earlier praise of urban places, a constant theme in commentary on them for thousands of years. A writer for *The Shanghai Star* asserted in 2002 that during the preceding decade, the newspaper had "charted the transformation of Shanghai from a third-world backwater into the world's most dynamic metropolis. . . . Over these 10 years the number of high-rise buildings in Puxi [West Shanghai] has increased more than tenfold, while Pudong [East Shanghai] has emerged out of swampy farmland to become one of the most spectacular cityscapes on Earth."[13] In 2008, Nick Land, the author of a guidebook, swooned over Shanghai, in the sort of language one can expect to read in such a publication: "The future that almost everyone will encounter eventually is first evident in dense, economically dynamic, cosmopolitan cities. Over its erratic history, Shanghai has certainly grasped more than its share of tomorrow . . . at the beginning of the 21st century it finds itself positioned once again on the outer edge of urban possibility, opening a window onto the emerging Asian Century and basking in international fascination."[14]

The Nigerian businessman Albert Okumagba has heaped praise on Lagos, the center of one of the two largest urban agglomerations in Africa. He refers enthusiastically to Lagos's thriving social scene, "fuelled by a representative melting pot of peerless and often timeless artists, poets, musicians, broadcasters, media practitioners and entertainment impresarios." He continues: "From our social clubs and parties to our ubiquitous places of worship the hard-working . . . swell of Lagosians are offered the opportunity to remind ourselves that a common humanity is what matters the most, even as we strive to make a living. I am convinced that this social cohesion is what has made Lagos . . . somehow defy the doubters and thrive, despite the many challenges it faces."[15] In this view, cultural vitality, a dynamic civil society, and fundamental unity all go together.

Finally, there is the rhetoric with regard to one of the two largest agglomerations in South America that appears on the website for the 2016 Rio Olympics:

> In its prime at over 400 years old . . . Brazil's current intellectual and cultural hub is working to deliver the greatest sports festival in the world. . . . Rio is widely known for its breathtaking landscapes and its people's unique joie de vivre. A combination of lakes, ocean and lush mountains marks the natural exuberance and typical colours of the Marvellous City. The friendliness of the cariocas (or "people born in Rio") can be witnessed in the streets, in bars and at the beach, where the sunset is a rare experience worth enjoying with an open heart by visitors and locals alike.[16]

In this perspective, Rio stands as an embodiment of the qualities that have long made cities centers of civilization and objects of admiration. At the same time, it points implicitly to some of the reasons why—despite cities' manifold defects and problems—people in search of better lives have chosen to live there.

As climate change accelerates, whether the numerous cities that adjoin ocean waters will retain their attractiveness or even their viability remains to be seen. What one can say in this connection is that acquiring the knowledge and inventing the techniques that will be necessary for combating the effects of global warming are most likely to occur in urban settings. As in the past, cities will continue to be the places where the future is shaped.

Chronology

CA. 10TH–4TH MILLENNIA BCE
Neolithic Revolution

CA. 3500 BCE
Emergence of Uruk and other cities in Mesopotamia

CA. 2500–1500 BCE
Cities in Indus River Valley flourish

CA. 1800–300 BCE
Early development of cities in China

CA. 1200–700 BCE
Phoenician cities reach their peak

CA. 700–600 BCE
Establishment of first cities in Mesoamerica

CA. 600 BCE
High point in the history of Babylon

5TH CENTURY BCE
Golden age in the history of Athens

332 BCE
Establishment of Alexandria

3RD CENTURY BCE
High point in the history of Pataliputra in India

202 BCE–220 CE
Han dynasty in China

27 BCE–14 CE
Reign of Caesar Augustus in Rome

324–330
Establishment of Constantinople

476
End of the Roman Empire in the West

CA. 570–632
Life of the Prophet Muhammad and beginning of the spread of Islam

8TH CENTURY
Flourishing of Chang'an in China

8TH AND 9TH CENTURIES
Apogee of Mayan cities

762
Establishment of Baghdad

CA.1000
Start of urban revival in Europe

1275
Arrival of Marco Polo in Beijing

1348
Black Death in Europe

15TH CENTURY
Golden age in the history of Florence

1453
Ottoman conquest of Constantinople

1497–1499
Voyage from Lisbon to India and back to Lisbon by Vasco da Gama

16TH CENTURY
Growth of Spanish and Portuguese presence in Latin America

1520
Spanish conquest of Tenochtitlán in Mexico

1590
Start of upsurge of Edo in Japan

1590s
Start of performance of plays written by William Shakespeare in London

17TH AND 18TH CENTURIES
Establishment of British colonies in North America

1643–1715
Reign of Louis XIV in France

1666
Great fire in London

CA. 1760
Start of the Industrial Revolution in
Britain

1776
Proclamation of the American
Declaration of Independence in
Philadelphia

1789
Outbreak of the French Revolution
in Paris

1800–1848
Onset of industrialization in Western
and Central Europe

1815–1914
High rates of European and American
urban growth

1848–1849
Revolutions on the European continent

CA. 1850–1914
Expanding roles of urban reformers and
municipal governments

1858
British government asserts formal
control over large parts of India

1868
Meiji Restoration in Japan and start of
period of modernization

CA. 1875–1914
Expansion of European control
in Africa

1914–1918
World War I

1917–1922
Revolutions and Civil War
in Russia

1931
Completion of Empire State Building in
New York City

1935
Start of construction of the
Moscow Metro

1939–1945
World War II

1941–1944
Siege of Leningrad

1945
Bombings of Dresden, Hiroshima, and
Nagasaki

1946–1997
End of European empires

1950
High point in the history of Detroit

1950–2013
Growth of Shanghai from 5.4 million to
17.8 million inhabitants

2000
Half of U.S. population lives
in suburbs

CA. 2000–PRESENT
Cities in developing countries
increasingly afflicted by air pollution

Notes

CHAPTER 1

1. James P. Pritchard, ed., *Ancient Near Eastern Texts Relating to the Old Testament*, 3rd ed. (Princeton, NJ: Princeton University Press, 1969), 73.
2. Herodotus, *The History of Herodotus*, George Rawlinson, trans. and ed. (New York: Appleton, 1885), Bk. 1, Ch. 178.
3. Quoted in Mason Hammond, *The City in the Ancient World* (Cambridge, MA: Harvard University Press, 1972), 73.
4. The Holy Bible, Ezekiel 27:4–7, 9.

CHAPTER 2

1. Thucydides, *The Peloponnesian War*, Crawley translation (New York: Modern Library, 1951), 104–105.
2. Plutarch, *The Lives of the Noble Grecians and Romans*, John Dryden, trans. (New York: Modern Library, 1951), 192.
3. Strabo, *Geography*, H. L. Jones, trans. (London: Heinemann 1949), Bk. XVII, Chapter 1.
4. Quoted in Donald R. Dudley, *Urbs Roma: A Source Book of Classical Texts on the City and Its Monuments* (Aberdeen, UK: University of Aberdeen Press, 1967), 16.
5. Quoted in Dudley, *Urbs Roma*, 16.
6. Suetonius, *The Lives of the Twelve Caesars*, Alexander Thomson, trans. (London: Bell, 1890), 359–360.
7. E. R. Evans, "India in Early Greek and Latin Literature," in *The Cambridge History of India*, Vol. 1, E. J. Repson, ed. (Cambridge, UK: Cambridge University Press, 1922), 411–412.
8. Quoted in N. Steinhardt, "China," in Peter Clark, ed., *The Oxford Handbook of Cities in World History* (Oxford, UK: Oxford University Press, 2013), 124.

CHAPTER 3

1. In Philip Schaff and Henry Wace, eds., *Nicene and Post-Nicene Fathers*, second series, Vol. 6 (Peabody, MA: Hendrickson, 1994), Letter 127.
2. Published on the Internet: Fordham University, "Medieval Sourcebook: Procopius: De Aedificis." http://legacy.fordham.edu/Halsall/source/procop-deaed1.asp.
3. G. de Villehardouin, *Chronicle of the Fourth Crusade*, Frank Marzials, trans. (London: Dent, 1908), 31.
4. Cited in Francoise Micheau, "Baghdad in the Abbasid Era: A Cosmopolitan and Multi-Confessional Capital," in Salma K. Jayyusi et al., eds., *The City in the Islamic World*, Vol. I (Leiden and Boston: Brill, 2008), 244.
5. Micheau, "Baghdad in the Abbasid Era," 232.
6. Quoted in Nancy Shatzman Steinhardt, *Chinese Imperial City Planning* (Honolulu: University of Hawaii Press, 1990), 155.

7. Quoted in Ignacio Bernal, "Mexico-Tenochtitlan," in Arnold Toynbee, ed., *Cities of Destiny* (New York: McGraw-Hill, 1967), 204.

8. Hernando Cortés, *5 Letters of Cortés to the Emperor, 1519–1526*, J. Bayard Morris, trans. (New York and London: Norton, n.d.), 86–90.

9. Quoted in P. Ruggiers, *Florence in the Age of Dante* (Norman, OK: University of Oklahoma Press, 1964), ix. See also Leonardo Bruni, *In Praise of Florence: The Praise of the City of Florence and an Introduction to Leonardo Bruni's Civil Humanism*, Alfred Scheepers, trans. and ed. (Amsterdam: Olive Press, 2005), 77–120.

10. Ruggiers, *Florence in the Age of Dante*, ix.

CHAPTER 4

1. From Orest and Patricia Ranum, eds., *The Century of Louis XIV* (New York: Macmillan, 1972), 215.

2. From Ranum, eds., *The Century of Louis XIV*, 197.

3. From Walter L. Arnstein, ed., *The Past Speaks: Sources and Problems in British History, Vol. II: Since 1688* (Lexington, MA: D. C. Heath, 1993), 37–38.

4. James Boswell, *Boswell's Life of Johnson*, Vol. 3, G. B. Hill, ed. (Oxford, UK: Clarendon Press, 1934), 178.

5. Louis-Sébastien Mercier, *Panorama of Paris*, Jeremy D. Popkin, ed. (University Park, PA: Pennsylvania State University Press, 1999), 28, 33.

6. Mercier, *Panorama of Paris*, 28, 33.

7. From Arnstein, ed., *The Past Speaks*, 43–44.

8. Engelbert Kaempfer, *Kaempfer's Japan: Tokugawa Culture Observed*, Beatrice M. Bodart-Bailey, trans. and ed. (Honolulu: University of Hawaii Press, 1999), 343–354. The central tower had burned down in 1657 and had not been rebuilt. Kaempfer probably consulted maps and guidebooks that showed the tower still located in the center of the castle when he wrote about it, suggesting that not all of his remarks were based on firsthand observation.

9. Cited in Maxwell S. Burt, *Philadelphia: Holy Experiment* (New York: Doubleday, 1945), 1–2.

10. Jacques-Louis Ménétra, *Journal of My Life*, Arthur Goldhammer, trans. (New York: Columbia University Press, 1986), 219.

CHAPTER 5

1. Robert Vaughan, *The Age of Great Cities: Or, Modern Society Viewed in Its Relation to Intelligence, Morals, and Religion* (London: Jackson and Walford, 1843), 1; Adna Weber, *The Growth of Cities in the Nineteenth Century: A Study in Statistics* (Ithaca, NY: Cornell University Press, 1899), 1, 7.

2. Quoted in Blair A. Ruble, *Second Metropolis: Pragmatic Pluralism in Gilded Age Chicago, Silver Age Moscow, and Meiji Osaka* (Cambridge, UK, and New York: Cambridge University Press, 2001), 112.

3. Friedrich Engels, *The Condition of the Working Classes in England*, W. O. Henderson and W. H. Chaloner, trans. and ed. (Stanford, CA: Stanford University Press, 1968), 75.

4. Quoted in Andrew Lees, *Cities Perceived: Urban Society in European and American Thought, 1820–1940* (New York: Columbia University Press, 1985), 73.

5. Quoted in Lees, *Cities Perceived*, 138.

6. Quoted in Charles N. Glaab and A. Theodore Brown, *A History of Urban America*, 2nd ed. (New York and London: Macmillan, 1976), 54.

7. Quoted in Lees, *Cities Perceived*, 170.

8. Vaughan, *The Age of Great Cities*, 296–297.

9. Quoted in Lees, *Cities Perceived*, 242.

10. Charles Zueblin, *American Municipal Progress*, 2nd ed. (New York: Macmillan, 1916), 401.

11. Frederic C. Howe, *The City: The Hope of Democracy* (New York: Scribner's, 1905), 25.

CHAPTER 6

1. "The Present Day," in *Twentieth Century Impressions of British Malaya*, Arnold Wright, ed. (London: Lloyd's Greater Britain Publishing Company, 1908), 117.

2. Quoted in Pankaj Mishra, *From the Ruins of Empire: The Intellectuals Who Remade Asia* (New York: Farrar, Straus, and Giroux, 2012), 36.

3. Quoted in William Dalrymple, *The Last Mogul: The Fall of a Dynasty: Delhi, 1857* (London: Bloomsbury, 2006), 364.

4. Quoted in Mishra, *From the Ruins of Empire*, 127.

5. Quoted in Asa Briggs, *Victorian Cities* (New York and Evanston, IL: Harper & Row, 1963), 283.

6. Quoted in Prashant Kidambi, *The Making of an Indian Metropolis: Colonial Governance and Public Culture in Bombay, 1880–1920* (Aldershot, UK: Ashgate, 2007), 23.

7. Quoted in Kidambi, *The Making of an Indian Metropolis*, 24.

8. Quoted in Kidambi, *The Making of an Indian Metropolis*, 49.

9. Quoted in Robert Home, *Of Planting and Planning: The Making of British Colonial Cities* (London: Spon, 1997), 78.

10. Quoted in Carl H. Nightingale, *Segregation: A Global History of Divided Cities* (Chicago and London: University of Chicago Press, 2012), 181.

11. Quoted in Home, *Of Planting and Planning*, 117.

12. Quoted in Anthony D. King, *Urbanism, Colonialism, and the World Economy: Cultural and Spatial Foundations of the World Urban System* (London and New York: Routledge, 1990), 44.

CHAPTER 7

1. Stefan Zweig, *The World of Yesterday*, Helmut Ripperger, trans. (New York: Viking Press, 1943), 223.

2. Quoted in Maureen Healy, *Vienna and the Fall of the Habsburg Empire: Total War and Everyday Life in World War I* (Cambridge, UK, and New York: Cambridge University Press, 2004), 61.

3. John Reed, *Ten Days That Shook the World* (New York: Modern Library, 1935), 257–258.

4. Timothy J. Colton, *Moscow: Governing the Socialist Metropolis* (Cambridge, MA: Harvard University Press, 1995), 267.

5. Cicely Hamilton, *Modern England, as Seen by an Englishwoman* (London: Dent, 1938), 173–174; Sydney Vere Pearson, *London's Overgrowth and the Causes of Swollen Towns* (London: Daniel, 1939), 9.

6. Quoted in Tom Harrison, *Living through the Blitz* (New York: Schocken Books, 1976), 95.

7. Quoted in Cynthia Simmons and Nina Perlina, *Writing the Siege of Leningrad: Women's Diaries, Memoirs, and Documentary Prose* (Pittsburgh, PA: University of Pittsburgh Press, 2002), 50–51.

8. Quoted in David Clay Large, *Berlin* (New York: Basic Books, 2000), 350.

9. Stephen Spender, *European Witness* (London: Hamish Hamilton, 1946), 14–17.

10. Quoted in Iris Chang, *The Rape of Nanking: The Forgotten Holocaust of World War II* (New York: Basic Books, 1997), 154.

11. Quoted in Haruko Taya Cook and Theodore F. Cook, *Japan at War: An Oral History* (New York: The New Press, 1992), 385.

12. Quoted in Jeffry M. Diefendorf, *In the Wake of War: The Reconstruction of German Cities after World War II* (New York and Oxford, UK: Oxford University Press, 1993), 63.

CHAPTER 8

1. Charlie LeDuff, *Detroit: An American Autopsy* (New York: Penguin, 2013), 4–5.

2. Robert Fishman, *Bourgeois Utopias: The Rise and Fall of Suburbia* (New York: Basic Books, 1987).

3. Jane Jacobs, *The Death and Life of Great American Cities* (New York: Vintage, 1963), 445–448.

4. Jeremy Seabrook, *In the Cities of the South: Scenes from a Developing World* (London and New York: Verso, 1996), 6, 10.

5. Mike Davis, *Planet of Slums* (London and New York, 2006), 19.

6. Quoted in Norma Evenson, *The Indian Metropolis: A View Toward the West* (New Haven, CT, and London: Yale University Press, 1989), 192–194.

7. Quoted in Alan Gilbert, "Poverty, Inequality, and Social Segregation," in Peter Clark, ed., *The Oxford Handbook of Cities in World History* (Oxford, UK: Oxford University Press, 2013), 686.

8. Davis, *Planet of Slums*, 146–147.

9. Thomas L. Friedman, "Too Big to Breathe?," *New York Times*, November 6, 2013, A23.

10. Friedman, "Too Big to Breathe?," 270–271.

11. Edward Glaeser, *The Triumph of the City: How Our Greatest Invention Makes Us Richer, Smarter, Greener, and Happier* (New York: Penguin Press, 2011), 7.

12. Glaeser, *The Triumph of the City*, 90.

13. Quoted in Jeffrey N. Wasserstrom, *Global Shanghai, 1850–2010: A History in Fragments* (London and New York: Routledge, 2009), 1.

14. Quoted in Wasserstrom, *Global Shanghai*, 124.

15. Albert Okumagba, "A Personal Message from the CEO of BGL," in Kaye Whiteman, *Lagos: A Cultural and Historical Companion* (Oxford, UK: Signal Books, 2012), xiii.

16. www.rio2016.org/en/rio-de-janeiro/rio-and-its-history.

Further Reading

GENERAL WORKS

Bairoch, Paul. *Cities and Economic Development: From the Dawn of History to the Present*, Christopher Braider, trans. Chicago: University of Chicago Press, 1988.

Birch, Eugenie L., and Susan M. Wachter, eds. *Global Urbanization.* Philadelphia: University of Pennsylvania Press, 2011.

Cassis, Youssef. *Capitals of Capital: The Rise and Fall of International Financial Centers, 1780–2009.* New York and Cambridge, UK: Cambridge University Press, 2006.

Chandler, Tertius, and Gerald Fox. *3000 Years of Urban Growth.* New York: Academic Press, 1974.

Clark, Peter, ed. *The Oxford Handbook of Cities in World History.* Oxford, UK: Oxford University Press, 2013.

Fishman, Robert. *Bourgeois Utopias: The Rise and Fall of Suburbia.* New York: Basic Books, 1987.

Glaeser, Edward. *The Triumph of the City: How Our Greatest Invention Makes Us Richer, Smarter, Greener, Healthier, and Happier.* New York: Penguin, 2011.

Hall, Peter. *Cities in Civilization: Culture, Innovation, and Urban Order.* London: Weidenfeld & Nicolson, 1998.

Hein, Carola, ed. *Port Cities: Dynamic Landscapes and Global Networks.* London: Routledge, 2011.

Mumford, Louis. *The City in History: Its Origins, Its Transformations, and Its Prospects.* New York: Harcourt, Brace, 1961.

Sassen, Saskia. *The Global City: New York, London, Tokyo.* Princeton, NJ: Princeton University Press, 1991.

Sutcliffe, Anthony. *Towards the Planned City: Germany, Britain, the United States and France, 1780–1914.* Oxford, UK: Blackwell, 1981.

Sutcliffe, Anthony, ed. *Metropolis, 1890–1940.* Chicago: University of Chicago Press, 1984.

Toynbee, Arnold, ed. *Cities of Destiny.* New York: McGraw-Hill, 1967.

Weber, Adna Ferrin. *The Growth of Cities in the Nineteenth Century: A Study in Statistics.* Ithaca, NY: Cornell University Press, 1899.

THE ANCIENT NEAR EAST AND THE ANCIENT MEDITERRANEAN

Hammond, Mason. *The City in the Ancient World.* Cambridge, MA: Harvard University Press, 1972.

Jones, Arnold Hugh Martin. *The Greek City from Alexander to Justinian.* Oxford, UK: Clarendon, 1966.

Laurence, Ray, et al. *The City in the Roman West, C. 250 B.C.–C. A.D. 250.* Cambridge, UK: Cambridge University Press, 2011.

Van de Mieroop, Marc. *The Ancient Mesopotamian City.* Oxford, UK: Clarendon, 1997.

ASIA AND AFRICA

Abu-Lughod, Janet. *Cairo: 1001 Years of the City Victorious*. Princeton, NJ: Princeton University Press, 1971.

Anderson, David M., and Richard Rathbone, eds. *Africa's Urban Past*. Portsmouth, NH: Heinemann, 2000.

Bergère, Marie-Claude. *Shanghai: China's Gateway to Modernity*. Stanford, CA: Stanford University Press, 2009.

Campanella, Thomas J. *The Concrete Dragon: China's Urban Revolution and What It Means for the World*. New York: Princeton Architectural Press, 2008.

Chandavarkar, Rajnarayan. *History, Culture and the Indian City*. Cambridge, UK, and New York: Cambridge University Press, 2009.

Dick, Howard, and Peter J. Rimmer, eds. *Cities, Transport & Communications: The Integration of Southeast Asia since 1850*. London: Palgrave Macmillan, 2003.

El-Sheshtawy, Yasser, ed. *The Evolving Arab City: Tradition, Modernity and Urban Development*. London: Routledge, 2008.

Evenson, Norma. *The Indian Metropolis: A View Towards the West*. New Haven, CT: Yale University Press, 1989.

Freund, Bill. *The African City: A History*. Cambridge, UK, and New York: Cambridge University Press, 2007.

Kidambi, Prashant. *The Making of an Indian Metropolis: Colonial Governance and Public Culture in Bombay, 1890–1920*. Aldershot, UK: Ashgate, 2007.

Lapidus, Ira M. *Muslim Cities in the Later Middle Ages*. Cambridge, MA: Harvard University Press, 1967.

Metcalf, Thomas. *An Imperial Vision: Indian Architecture and Britain's Raj*. Berkeley, CA: University of California Press, 1989.

Read, Anthony. *Southeast Asia in the Age of Commerce, 1450–1680*, 2 vols. New Haven, CT: Yale University Press, 1988–1993.

Seabrook, Jeremy. *In the Cities of the South: Scenes from a Developing World*. London and New York: Verso, 1996.

Skinner, G. William, ed. *The City in Late Imperial China*. Stanford, CA: Stanford University Press, 1977.

Sorensen, André. *The Making of Urban Japan: Cities and Planning from Edo to the Twenty-first Century*. London: Routledge, 2004.

Steinhardt, Nancy Shatzman. *Chinese Imperial City Planning*. Honolulu: University of Hawaii Press, 1990.

Wright, Gwendolyn. *The Politics of Design in French Colonial Urbanism*. Chicago: University of Chicago Press, 1991.

EUROPE

Briggs, Asa. *Victorian Cities*. Berkeley, CA: University of California Press, 1993.

Brower, Daniel R. *The Russian City between Tradition and Modernity, 1850–1900*. Berkeley, CA: University of California Press, 1990.

Bucholz, Robert O., and Joseph P. Ward. *London: A Social and Cultural History, 1550–1750*. Cambridge, UK, and New York: Cambridge University Press, 2012.

Clark, Peter. *European Cities and Towns, 400–2000*. Oxford, UK: Oxford University Press, 2009.

Clark, Peter, ed. *The Cambridge Urban History of Britain, Volume II: 1540–1840*. Cambridge, UK, and New York: Cambridge University Press, 2000.

Cohen, William B. *Urban Government and the Rise of the French City: Five Municipalities in the Nineteenth Century*. New York: St. Martin's, 1998.

Colton, Timothy. *Moscow: Governing the Socialist Metropolis*. Cambridge, MA: Harvard University Press, 1995.

Daunton, Martin, ed. *The Cambridge Urban History of Britain, Volume III: 1840–1950*. Cambridge, UK, and New York: Cambridge University Press, 2000.

De Vries, Jan. *European Urbanization, 1500–1800*. Cambridge, MA: Harvard University Press, 1984.

Diefendorf, Jeffry, ed. *Rebuilding Europe's Bombed Cities*. New York: St. Martin's, 1990.

Diefendorf, Jeffry. *In the Wake of War: The Reconstruction of German Cities after World War II*. New York: Oxford University Press, 1993.

Evenson, Norma. *Paris: A Century of Change*. New Haven, CT: Yale University Press, 1979.

Friedrichs, Christopher R. *The Early Modern City, 1450–1750*. London: Longman, 1995.

Garrioch, David. *The Making of Revolutionary Paris*. Berkeley, CA, and Los Angeles: University of California Press, 2002.

Hamm, Michael F., ed. *The City in Russian History*. Lexington, KY: The University Press of Kentucky, 1976.

Hohenberg, Paul M., and Lynn Hollen Lees. *The Making of Urban Europe, 1000–1994*. Cambridge, MA: Harvard University Press, 1995.

Hunt, Tristram. *Building Jerusalem: The Rise and Fall of the Victorian City*. New York: Holt, 2005.

Koven, Seth R. *Slumming: Sexual and Social Politics in Victorian London*. Princeton, NJ: Princeton University Press, 2004.

Ladd, Brian. *The Ghosts of Berlin: Confronting German History in the Urban Landscape*. Chicago: University of Chicago Press, 1997.

Ladd, Brian. *Urban Planning and Civic Order in Germany, 1860–1914*. Cambridge, MA: Harvard University Press, 1990.

Lees, Andrew, and Lynn Hollen Lees. *Cities and the Making of Modern Europe, 1750–1914*. Cambridge, UK, and New York: Cambridge University Press, 2007.

Lenger, Friedrich. *European Cities in the Modern Era, 1850–1914*, Joel Golb, trans. Leiden, NE, and Boston: Brill, 2012.

Nicholas, David. *The Growth of the Medieval City: From Late Antiquity to the Early Fourteenth Century*. New York: Longman, 1997.

Nicholas, David. *The Later Medieval City, 1300–1500*. London and New York: Longman, 1997.

Palliser, D. M., ed. *The Cambridge Urban History of Britain, Volume I: 600–1540*. Cambridge, UK, and New York: Cambridge University Press, 2000.

Porter, Roy. *London: A Social History*. Cambridge, MA: Harvard University Press, 1994.

Roth, Ralf, and Marie-Noëlle Polino, eds. *The City and the Railway in Europe*. Burlington, VT: Ashgate, 2003.

Winter, Jay, and Jean-Louis Robert, eds. *Capital Cities at War: Paris, London, Berlin, 1914–1919,* 2 vols. Cambridge, UK, and New York: Cambridge University Press, 1997–2007.

THE AMERICAS

Abbott, Carl. *How Cities Won the West: Four Centuries of Urban Change in Western North America.* Albuquerque, NM: University of New Mexico Press, 2008.

Boyer, Paul S. *Urban Masses and Moral Order in America, 1820–1920.* Cambridge, MA: Harvard University Press, 1978.

Davis, Diane E. *Urban Leviathan: Mexico City in the Twentieth Century.* Philadelphia: Temple University Press, 1994.

Gilbert, Alan G. *The Latin American City.* London and New York: Monthly Review Press, 1998.

Goldfield, David R., ed. *Encyclopedia of American Urban History,* 2 vols. Thousand Oaks, CA: Sage, 2007.

Goldfield, David R., and Blaine A. Brownell. *Urban America: From Downtown to No Town.* Boston: Houghton Mifflin, 1979.

Greenfield, Gerald Michael, ed. *Latin American Urbanization: Historical Profiles of Major Cities.* Westport, CT: Greenwood, 1994.

Hayden, Dolores. *Building Suburbia: Green Fields and Urban Growth, 1820–2000.* New York: Vintage, 2003.

Kinsbruner, Jay. *The Colonial Spanish American City: Urban Life in the Age of Atlantic Capitalism.* Austin, TX: University of Texas Press, 2005.

Kruse, Kevin, and Thomas J. Sugrue, eds. *The New Suburban History.* Chicago: University of Chicago Press, 2006.

Lemon, James T. *Liberal Dreams and Nature's Limits: Great Cities of North America since 1600.* Oxford, UK, and New York: Oxford University Press, 1986.

Nash, Gary. *The Urban Crucible: The Northern Seaports and the American Revolution.* Cambridge, MA: Harvard University Press, 1986.

URBAN CULTURAL LIFE AND REPRESENTATIONS

Bender, Thomas. *New York Intellect: A History of Intellectual Life in New York City: From 1750 to the Beginnings of Our Own Time.* New York: Knopf, 1987.

Byrd, Max. *London Transformed: Images of the City in the Eighteenth Century.* New Haven, CT, and London: Yale University Press, 1978.

Coleman, B. I., ed. *The Idea of the City in Nineteenth-Century Britain.* London and Boston: Routledge, 1973.

Dennis, Richard. *Cities in Modernity: Representations and Productions of Metropolitan Space, 1840–1930.* Cambridge, UK, and New York: Cambridge University Press, 2008.

Dougherty, James. *The Fivesquare City: The City in the Religious Imagination.* Notre Dame, IN, and London: University of Notre Dame Press, 1980.

Dyos, H. J., and Michael Wolff, eds. *The Victorian City: Images and Realities,* 2 vols. London and Boston: Routledge, 1973.

Fishman, Robert. *Urban Utopias in the Twentieth Century: Ebenezer Howard, Frank Lloyd Wright, Le Corbusier.* New York: Basic Books, 1977.

Fritzsche, Peter. *Reading Berlin: 1900.* Cambridge, MA: Harvard University Press, 1996.

Hamer, David. *New Towns in the New World: Images and Perceptions of the Nineteenth-Century Urban Frontier.* New York: Columbia University Press, 1990.

Lees, Andrew. *Cities Perceived: Urban Society in European and American Thought, 1820–1940.* New York: Columbia University Press, 1985.

Lehan, Richard. *The City in Literature: An Intellectual and Cultural History.* Berkeley, CA: University of California Press, 1998.

Schwartz, Vanessa. *Spectacular Realities: Early Mass Culture in Fin-de-Siècle Paris.* Berkeley, CA, and Los Angeles: University of California Press, 1998.

Seigel, Jerrold. *Bohemian Paris.* New York: Viking, 1986.

Spears, Timothy. *Chicago Dreaming: Midwesterners and the City, 1871–1919.* Chicago: University of Chicago Press, 2005.

Steinberg, Mark D. *Petersburg Fin de Siècle.* New Haven, CT: Yale University Press, 2011.

Storoni Mazzolani, Lidia. *The Idea of the City in Roman Thought*, S. O'Donnell, trans. Bloomington, IN: University of Indiana Press, 1970.

White, Morton, and Lucia White. *The Intellectual versus the City: From Thomas Jefferson to Frank Lloyd Wright.* Cambridge, MA: Harvard University Press, 1962.

Websites

Berlin
www.berlin.de/en/
An official site of the German capital. Provides detailed narratives of the history of Berlin in English, as well as in German, beginning with "The Medieval Trading Center" and ending with "The New Berlin."

British History Online
www.british-history.ac.uk/catalogue/london
Contains hundreds of primary sources and maps that pertain to the British capital. Site based at the Institute of Historical Research, University of London.

Cleveland Historical
www.clevelandhistorical.org
Offers dozens of virtual tours of the city, focusing on historic places and buildings. Also provides hundreds of stories about events in Cleveland's past. Developed by the Center for Public History and Digital Humanities at Cleveland State University.

Encyclopedia of Chicago
www.encyclopedia.chicagohistory.org
An easily searchable collection of entries that pertain to the great Midwestern metropolis, maintained by the Chicago Historical Society. Many primary sources, maps, and other illustrations.

The Encyclopedia of Greater Philadelphia
www.philadelphiaencyclopedia.org
Developed by the Mid-Atlantic Regional Center for the Humanities at Rutgers-Camden. Contains numerous essays, maps, and other illustrations that pertain to the area's history. Begins prior to colonization and reaches up to the present. Featured subjects range from "Activism" to "Women."

European Association for Urban History
www.eauh.eu
A bibliography on this website lists recent collections of essays that have grown out of conferences of the association held since 1994. It also lists a dozen journals that focus on various aspects of urban history.

Go Tokyo
www.gotokyo.org/search/en/genre
An official Tokyo travel guide. Numerous illustrations and descriptions of several types of buildings constructed in the city over many centuries, with emphasis on temples, shrines, and other public structures.

Marvellous Melbourne Museum Victoria
www.museumvictoria.com.au/marvellous
Narratives and pictures pertaining to the history of an Australian metropolis from the 1830s through the 1950s.

Museum of London
www.museumoflondonprints.org.uk
Ten "permanent galleries," arranged chronologically, are described and illustrated. Via *www.londonmuseumprints.com*, one can bring up thousands of images, among them posters, photographs, paintings, maps, and other prints that illustrate all periods in the history of the British metropolis.

**NYC History Sources
on the Web**
*www.virtualny.cuny.edu/resources.
html*

Provides links to sixteen other
websites that illuminate various
aspects of New York's past, among
them "Ellis Island," "Forgotten
New York," "Great Buildings," and
"The September 11 Digital Archive."
Produced by the New Media Lab
at the Graduate Center of the City
University of New York.

**Virtual Museum of the City
of San Francisco**
www.sfmuseum.org

Contains information on numerous
topics in the city's history, with
particular attention to the gold rush,
the great fire and earthquake of
1906, and the Golden Gate Bridge.
Includes copious primary sources
and illustrations. Site maintained
by the Museum of the City of San
Francisco.

Acknowledgments

I am indebted in the first place to my Rutgers colleague Bonnie Smith for having asked me to write this book for The New Oxford World History series and for her comments, encouragement, and suggestions during the past several years.

I owe a very large collective debt of gratitude to my good friend Peter Clark and the dozens of contributors whom he recruited for the massive *Oxford Handbook of Cities in World History* (2013). My work was greatly facilitated by the information and interpretations presented by these fellow scholars. Their efforts have resulted in an in-depth survey of urban history from ancient times to the present, and I regret that I cannot name them all here. One contributor to Peter's volume I do want to mention is Niko Lipsanen. He produced twenty excellent regional maps, four of which appear in slightly modified form in this book.

The entire manuscript was read and carefully commented on by several scholars, among them Marc Boone, a second reader for Oxford University Press, and Craig Lockard. Their suggestions were particularly useful with regard to what I wrote about developments outside the areas of modern Europe and the United States.

Several historians at Rutgers-Camden and elsewhere also provided valuable help. Gerry Verbrugghe carefully scrutinized my first three chapters and thereby saved me from a number of errors. Nick Kapur, Charlene Mires, and Lorrin Thomas answered questions on the basis of expertise in areas about which I know little, as did Joan Neuberger and Nancy Steinhardt. John Gibson of the Rutgers–Camden Robeson Library did an excellent job of making digital copies of pictures that had appeared in books.

At Oxford University Press, both Nancy Toff and Karen Fein worked constantly to push me toward making my prose accessible to a broad audience of readers. Kate Nunn expertly guided my work through the production process.

As always, my greatest debt is to Lynn Hollen Lees, an accomplished urban historian who has been my scholarly partner, as well as my cherished wife, for over fifty years.

Index

NEW OXFORD WORLD HISTORY

 The
New
Oxford
World
History

GENERAL EDITORS

BONNIE G. SMITH,
Rutgers University
ANAND A. YANG,
University of Washington

EDITORIAL BOARD

DONNA GUY,
Ohio State University
KAREN ORDAHL KUPPERMAN,
New York University
MARGARET STROBEL,
University of Illinois, Chicago
JOHN O. VOLL,
Georgetown University

The New Oxford World History
provides a comprehensive, synthetic
treatment of the "new world
history" from chronological,
thematic, and geographical
perspectives, allowing readers to
access the world's complex history
from a variety of conceptual,
narrative, and analytical viewpoints
as it fits their interests.

Andrew Lees is Distinguished
Professor of History at Rutgers
University in Camden. He is the
author of *Cities and the Making of
Modern Europe, 1750–1914* (2007),
*Cities, Sin, and Social Reform
in Imperial Germany* (2002),
*Cities Perceived: Urban Society in
European and American Thought,
1820–1940* (1985), and *Revolution
and Reflection: Intellectual Change
in Germany during the 1850s*
(1974). He is the editor of *Character
Is Destiny: The Autobiography
of Alice Salomon, 1872–1948*
(2004) and co-editor of *The Rise
of Urban Britain* (1985) and *The
Urbanization of European Society in
the Nineteenth Century* (1976).